Enjoy Your Teenagers

Enjoy Your Teenagers

Jean Robb and Hilary Letts

Hodder & Stoughton
LONDON SYDNEY AUCKLAND

British Library Cataloguing in Publication Data
A record for this book is available from the British Library

ISBN 0 340 78577 2

Typeset by Avon Dataset Ltd, Bidford-on-Avon, Warks

Printed and bound in Great Britain by
The Guernsey Press Co. Ltd, Channel Isles

Hodder & Stoughton
A Division of Hodder Headline Ltd
338 Euston Road
London NW1 3BH

To Adam and Matthew, teenagers past,
and Natasha and Karina, teenagers of the future

Contents

Introduction

Use this book to find ways to delight in your teenagers and your life! It may surprise you to discover that a self-help book which has been written to help parents enjoy their teenagers also includes ways for parents to help themselves. It has been written as a source of help and advice you can turn to in the same way you would turn to a trusted and sympathetic friend. Go to it for practical support, comfort, common sense and nurturing.

Enjoy Your Teenagers will help you discover ways to keep a sense of perspective about your teenagers. You will be reminded about how important it is to look after yourself. You will see it makes sense to work on something you can improve – your own well-being – when trying to find the way to support your offspring in their teenage years. You will come to know that, whatever you are involved in and whatever problems you are facing, being fit will enable you to handle challenges much more effectively.

Just as when you talk to a trusted friend you get a chance to see things differently, this book gives you the opportunity to bounce ideas around. You can choose the ideas that appeal to you and you feel comfortable to try. You can put to one side any ideas that don't seem helpful now but could be later.

Take a holistic approach to your family life. You as a parent, as well as your teenagers, will be going through your own personal changes. All members of the family need to be motivated, able to cope with disappointments and difficulties, and deal with everyday life. Adults can feel they are faced with similar problems to teenagers, but teenage problems seem to stand out stark and unsurmountable because, for teenagers, they are being faced for the first time.

It would be pointless for us to tell you to tell your teenagers what to do. It might make the situation worse! But what is worth our while is helping you to learn how to look at different situations as they arise. You will see how to think about the situations you want to improve so you can increase the amount of time you spend enjoying your teenagers and cut down on the number of times when you might feel anger, regret, guilt or disappointment.

No matter what age your children are, if you as parents are not handling problems well your children will find life tricky too. All of us function better if we give ourselves space to think. Open *Enjoy Your Teenagers* on any page and find out how to help them cope.

1

It's not all sex, drugs and rock and roll

So you've got a teenager

We believe that life with teenagers may be as rewarding as other parts of your life. We believe parents need ideas and comfort. In this book we provide practical ideas, solace and strength. This book can give you a chance for a fresh start.

Teenagers can swing in and out of feelings faster than any one of us can imagine. One minute you are having a friendly chat and the next the teenager has stormed out full of woe because you don't understand.

This book:

- provides you with ways of coping with and enjoying your teenagers.
- tries not to stereotype teenagers. We have chosen instead to explore how parents can enjoy the teenage years rather than feel shattered by them.
- will help you think through why you feel the way you do and how you can put your thoughts and feelings across to those you care about.

3

- will help you put your thoughts and feelings across to those you hope can help you.
- will help you talk with teenagers about your concerns.
- will remind you of the power of praise.

Life with teenagers is not always easy

Teenagers can feel:

- despondent
- reckless
- irresponsible
- isolated
- betrayed.

These feelings are part of the struggle to grow from a child into an adult.

Teenagers can also feel:

- euphoric
- confident
- special
- loved
- loving.

These feelings are part of growing up too. This book helps you cope with mood swings, yours and theirs.

This book will help you to understand what sort of parent you want to be. It will help you realize that there is no one way of being a parent. It will give you the confidence and the strategies to change something if it is not working. It will show you how to look at what you are doing and see if you can do it differently.

Most importantly this book will help you realize that most teenagers grow up to be adults who can cope.

Deep trouble

There are many programmes and places where parents can get up-to-date information on the latest research, therapies and support for teenagers who are experiencing serious and possibly damaging conditions. Therapies change and parents can seek alternative and mainstream treatment to help their teenagers. We don't provide expert advice on these therapies or severe disorders. We have included the addresses of some recognized centres of help in the book.

Our expertise comes from working with teenagers over many years. We are expert in dealing with teenage problems that drive adults mad or make them feel incompetent.

Information to go

Teenage magazines cover many subjects close to the hearts and minds of teenagers in a teenage-friendly manner. Television programmes often provide information in an accessible way. There are drop-in centres for teenagers where teenagers can feel safe to speak about their fears and be given other places where they can get help.

Drop-in centres are there because young people need adult guidance. Sometimes they are too confused or embarrassed to ask their parents first. Some teenagers want to talk about everything to their parents. Other teenagers, even teenagers in the same family, feel more private and prefer to go to an anonymous source to try and find out what they need to know.

Some dos and don'ts for how to enjoy teenagers

- Do recognize that the teenagers you care about are not clones of you.
- Do rejoice when things they have planned work.
- Do rejoice when things you have planned work.
- Do remember *always* that your children are separate from you.
- Do feel good that your teenagers are growing up.
- Do remember always that your teenagers love you and need your love.

- Do be easy on yourself or anyone else when your teenagers disappoint you.
- Do remember to praise.
- Don't waste your energy feeling guilty about the fact you are human and not perfect.

Where do feelings come from?

- Your own past history.
- Your expectations of what should be happening.
- What you feel you should be doing.
- What you are expecting from other people.
- Your physical condition.

As a parent you might feel:

ambitious	fulfilled	satisfied
competent	guilty	self-obsessed
complacent	involved	terrified
detached	lucky	tested
determined	over-powered	treacherous
defiant	over-powering	undervalued
exhilarated	proud	weepy
focused	reluctant	wishy-washy.

Thinking through your feelings

Quite often when your teenagers have a problem you feel overwhelmed by it and allow it to take over every aspect of your life. It is important to decide which bits of your life you are going to let the problem affect.

When you give time to think about it you will see which parts of your life are affected by the problem and which parts aren't. You will see which parts of your life need to be affected by the problem and which ones don't. You can then make sure that the parts that need to be affected are the only ones being affected.

Some people see parenting as 100 per cent involvement. They enjoy taking their teenagers to their activities, having their friends around and having heart-to-heart discussions. When things are going well not every parent wishes to parent in this way.

When a teenager has a problem most parents feel obliged to show their parenting credentials by devoting 100 per cent of their time, energy and thought to actions and activities to sort out the problem. This is completely normal but there needs to come a point where less involvement is offered. You can't live your teenagers' lives for them. Only rarely will parents need to offer 100 per cent support over an extended period.

It is so much easier when they aren't your own teenagers

Most parents say that it is easier to deal with other parents' teenagers than their own. This is because their reactions to other people's teenagers tend to be quite simple.

With your own teenagers you invest time, effort, money, your philosophy, your own experience and wisdom. With somebody else's teenager you will probably only have invested some time. It will have been a temporary investment. The feelings that arise from that involvement will be short lived. The teenagers have their own homes to return to.

With your own teenager you will have invested so much over such a long period that your feelings will run deep. Parents can be gripped by feelings they didn't even know they had or were capable of having. Some of those feelings are directly related to being parents but many are related to being the individuals they are. You are living with your teenagers and see them nearly every day. You will be aware of your feelings most of the time.

What sort of parent did you hope you would be?

Think back to the time before you even had children. Did you think what sort of parent you would be? Did you hope you would be:

7

relaxed   a fun playmate
jolly   full of helpful and useful information
competent   a friend to confide in?

What words sum up the way you feel about yourself as a parent now?

bad tempered   shocked
exhausted   successful
confused   calm.
taken for granted

Free yourself to live your life

It is okay to find things about teenagers difficult to handle.

It is okay to have negative thoughts about teenagers.

Free yourself to live your life and learn how to move on from those negative feelings.

The first step is . . .

1. Identify your negative feelings

What is it that you feel when you think about your teenagers and you are feeling negative?

criticised   fed up   nervous
bewildered   hostile   out of your depth
inadequate   ignorant   despairing.

You might have all of these feelings or none of them. Add different ones to the list. Make the list your own. Your feelings are important. When you can think of exactly how you are feeling you will stand a better chance of freeing yourself from the feeling. The second step is . . .

2. Use words to liberate your thoughts

Without words we can't think clearly. A great deal of stress comes when we feel trapped. We know something is wrong but we have no words to describe it. We have to suffer. We can't do anything else.

Write down what you think, no matter how hideous, rude or uncaring it appears. Don't worry about writing in sentences, just words will do. As you look at what you have written try and think why those words have come into your mind. You might be appalled at what you have written but it is better to know exactly what is causing you to react the way you are. It is not treachery for parents to be angry with their teenagers and feel that they don't like them. It is not a betrayal to feel shocked by the way your teenagers are making you feel. It is not strange for parents to be bewildered by their teenagers yet want to be immersed in their lives. It is not unusual for parents to feel uncertain about what they should do next.

Step three is . . .

3. Clarify your thoughts
Once you begin to explore what you feel you can unlock where those feelings are coming from and then you can deal with them.

Making a fresh start

Sometimes when we look at lists about what we think or feel, we realize that what is happening in our lives is not what we want. It is possible to make a fresh start. It is worth making a fresh start. This book will show you how fresh starts are possible in many situations.

Fresh starts mean that you feel:

creative	released
communicative	clear
energized	purposeful
strong	you have greater understanding
confident	optimistic.

Be realistic about fresh starts
What is possible and realistic now may not be possible and realistic later.

What is possible and realistic now may not have been possible or realistic earlier.

When you make a fresh start, begin by thinking about what is possible and realistic now and for you.

Changing your situation

The important thing with a fresh start is that you take a new position. A small change can mean that you see the whole world quite differently from the way you did before.

Habits can hold you up

To make the small change takes less energy than you think. You will need to learn how to break a habit. You have to want things to change. It does take commitment.

People are surprised when they realize that the way they react to things is driven by habit not because of what is happening. They haven't realized that if they change their habit they can change everything.

Habit spotting – I knew she'd say that!

Habits might make us boring, unpopular or irritating but we often don't know how to stop them. Sometimes we don't even realize that it is a habit that is making us behave in a certain way. We are used to what we do and justify what we are doing as perfectly reasonable.

It is easier to spot habits in other people. Think of friends, relatives or work colleagues whom you try to avoid in certain situations because you know exactly what their reactions will be.

Habits can seem helpful – I love it when she says that

Of course not all habitual ways of responding to a situation are negative. Most people, even those who irritate us sometimes, have habits that make them appealing at other times. People seek out their company; their friendship or their help at particular times of need because they know the response they will get will be helpful.

Habit stopping – I hate it when she says that

Next time something happens that has upset you and you know that you have been upset in exactly the same way before, you have spotted a habit. At first you might feel that you are trapped. You think that there is no change that you could make or that you should make. However, if you don't want to be upset in exactly the same way again you must decide to make a change. You could:

- ask someone else what he or she would do in the same situation.
- think whether you have read about or seen someone else handle this situation.
- list what it is that makes you feel so upset and then see which things in the list you could change.

Remember you only need to change one thing for everything about your reaction to change. You can make a fresh start.

A fresh start can be made at any time

If every night when you come home from work you feel you are walking into the same nightmare of family squabbles, you can make a fresh start. You could:

- walk around the block once before you go in. As you walk notice the things around you – the stars, the gardens, the street signs, the people.

or:

- let the family know you will be listening to music for five minutes in a room on your own so you can wind down from your journey home.

or:

- have a shower and change your clothes as soon as you get in.

or:

- give someone else the opportunity to have a break.

These suggestions, or any others you might think of yourself, give you time to make sure you've changed your pace so you can meet any demands in a calm and relaxed state. When you are in a relaxed state you hear things and respond to things more calmly. You will be able to think more clearly about the order in which things can be done. You won't be as irritated when you can't control what is happening. You will be more realistic about what you can do.

Fresh starts for everyone

Building up a repertoire of fresh starts for yourself and your family can reduce the number of times you want to scream or turn round and go straight back to work.

As you practise the everyday fresh starts you will learn skills that will help you spot how to think of fresh starts for more challenging circumstances.

Fresh starts that work

Try:

- varying the pace;
- changing the activity;
- altering the sequence;
- rearranging the timing.

Most people reading this book will be using fresh starts automatically through their day. When we are handling things successfully we automatically put in fresh starts to keep the situation dynamic and fluid.

Change the tune

It is only when we hit a problem that we forget the importance of keeping the situation fresh. When you hear yourself speaking as if you are a recording you know that something needs to change. Equally if you hear others speaking as though they are recordings you need ways to get them out of the groove.

Have a laugh

Mike decided to have a shower as soon as he got home from work. He was amazed at the impact just having a shower had. When he joined the family his head felt clear. He felt comfortable and found himself laughing at his son's jokes.

A walk in the park

Sarah got off the bus so she could walk home through the park. By the time she got home her shoulders felt relaxed and the bounce had come back into her step. As she walked through the door she felt she was someone who enjoyed walking. Putting time aside for herself meant she had time to see herself differently. She became happier to give time to others. Previously she had felt that life was one long round of doing things for other people with no one doing anything for her.

Hobbies can help

When Freya's husband was unwell and needed constant care she gave up her job to be with him. At first she felt desperate because she had no control over her time. Her husband was often sleeping, but she didn't know when he would wake up. When he was awake she wanted to be there and was pleased that she could be there. When he wasn't awake she still wanted to have something to do. She started to sketch flowers that she picked from the garden. She had forgotten how much she enjoyed sketching. She appreciated the time to spend on developing her art. She found her mind expanding beyond the room she was in. She became alert and enthusiastic once again.

Café society

When Jean realized that her teenagers didn't enjoy her company she felt very stressed. When they were younger the family had all enjoyed being together. Now she seemed constantly to want more of their time than they wanted or were able to give her. She became more stressed. She could hear a whinge coming into her voice no matter what she said to them. She didn't seem able to control the whine, no matter how hard she tried. Jean eventually realized that the problem was she was lonely. It was company she wanted and she had time to do something about it. She rang an old friend and they started meeting at a bookshop that had a café. The whinge went out of Jean's voice when she spoke to her children. She had stopped feeling lonely. She had stopped feeling bitter about her family growing up.

At work
Office tensions were threatening productivity. Peter suggested that if the seating arrangements changed it might help.

It was like a miracle.

- people became more interesting;
- there seemed to be more energy;
- new relationships developed;
- communication improved;
- resentments disappeared;
- networking increased;
- people were happier to ask for help;
- people were able to identify ways of improving the working environment;
- the carpet was replaced;
- the photocopier was moved;
- and there was room for a water dispenser.

At home
Danny's family always sat in the same place at the dining table. They decided to change. Everyone was looking at someone different and something different. The conversation changed. The atmosphere changed. The family seemed more interested in what each other had to say. The relationships changed. Individuals had a chance to notice the body language of other members of the family and see and react to facial expressions they hadn't seen before.

You can feel a different person by making a simple change
You will feel:

- flexible
- adaptable
- interested
- inquisitive
- fresh
- positive.

Change versus wait and see

If you choose to change the way things are, you have more chance of being in step with real life than if you try to stop the change or ignore it. The rate of change in the world is fast and furious. The rate of change at home when you have teenagers is just as fast and furious but sometimes more difficult to see. Change doesn't have to wash over you. You don't have to be left out or feel out of step. You can understand the change game as well. You can manage to change. Change can be managed.

When to change

The time to change is when you feel:

- out of control;
- disappointed in yourself;
- confused by people's reactions;
- ignorant;
- exhausted.

Why changing matters so much

For those living with teenagers it can feel as if the only sure thing is that something is about to change. Being a teenager often seems to be all about changing. From hair colour to career choice the possibilities are endless, the choices overwhelming and the chopping and changing pretty constant. Parents can feel dazed and dismissed as their teenagers change.

Parents who are able to make positive changes for themselves will feel more relaxed about the changes in their teenagers. Making a positive change for yourself helps you see yourself in a new light.

Seeing yourself in a new light leads you to see others in a new light as well. Parenting teenagers is quite different from parenting the pre-teens. Coming to terms with that change can be one of the hardest experiences many parents will have to cope with.

Your teenagers don't always need you

It comes as quite a shock to teenagers to find their parents don't know everything.

It comes as quite a shock to parents to find that what they know isn't what their teenagers want or need to know.

Don't panic. You haven't done anything wrong. Teenagers want to start investigating the world for themselves. They will be excited by all the possibilities. They will love the feeling of power they get when they go to explore something new.

They no longer need you to introduce them to the world. They can do that for themselves. They can:

- talk to other people
- read information
- log on to the Internet
- travel
- watch TV.

New people will be important to them. New ideas will be fascinating to them. New experiences will be available to them.

You are still necessary to them but now it is on their terms.

The tender trap

It can be painful to watch teenagers take on life on their terms. We would like to protect them, have them always happy, always successful, always popular, always healthy and always safe. That, however, is not realistic. Very few adults live lives like that. Even fewer live them all through their adulthood.

Parents often get caught in the tender trap. They have enjoyed the role of parent to a younger child. They have felt needed and necessary. Up until now they have been the interface between their child and the outside world. Now it is time to move on. It is unnecessary for parents to prolong the role of caring for a young child beyond the age where their child needs that sort of care. It can delay or destroy the teenager's chance to grow up. It can look like caring but can be counter-productive.

The teenage years are when mature people, including parents and teachers, help the teenager realize that good days are not a right. Life is not necessarily fair. Life is unpredictable. When teenagers learn how to deal with the normal ups and downs that happen every day and to everyone, the happier they will be with the life they are living.

2

The teenage minefield

Tricky times with teenagers

Life with teenagers, like life in general, can be challenging, but there are ways of negotiating a way through tricky times. A tricky time is one where you feel uncertain about what is going on and whether you can cope. It can be when you believe that your teenager should be doing something in a particular way and he or she isn't. It can be when you think the world should be responding to your teenager in a particular way and it isn't.

Times when you feel like this can be fascinating. You can feel as though this is a challenge that you will be able to sort out if you just take time to think it through.

Times when you feel like this can be terrible. You can feel as though you are letting your teenager down and your teenager will never recover from this failing on your part.

When you feel terrible you need to take a deep breath and think again. This sounds impossible but the more stressed you get about the situation and the more driven you are to find a solution the less likely you are to find a way out.

Letting go

Letting go means that you stop trying to force the situation to be the way you want it to be. When you let go you can accept that:

- You can't always be on the same wavelength as your teenager or those who are trying to help your teenager.
- Something you said will be remembered.
- Something you said may be misunderstood.
- Something you said will be forgotten.
- You can't always sort out a problem with the first solution you think of.
- You can't predict what might happen.
- Every time you want to talk to your teenagers they may not want to talk to you.
- When your teenagers want to talk to you, you might not want to listen.
- It is not always as easy to sort out teenage problems as it is to sort out problems for young children.
- You won't be able to solve all their problems.
- People might not take the good advice you give.
- They may not know the advice you give is good advice.
- All the advice you give may not be good advice.

Learning to let go: be your own life coach

Everything we know we have learned. Not everything we learn from someone else is helpful. Not everything we learn by ourselves is true. We need to let go of the unhelpful and untrue things we have learned so that we can use what we know to help us cope with life optimistically. We can have the courage to fail. We can have the knowledge that there is always something to look forward to. There is life even after a disaster.

Praise yourself

There are some things we do that no one will ever notice. It is important that we are all able to feel pleasure in our own efforts. People who are too critical of their own efforts can be their own worst enemy. They either set unrealistic standards for themselves or can't believe that they are someone who can ever get anything right.

Feeling pleased with what you have done is not about boasting or showing off. It is about noticing the effort you have put in. It is also about being prepared to accept that you are not perfect. It is about recognizing that effort is worth praising, progress is worth praising and achievement is worth praising. It is about knowing that if other people haven't noticed that does not mean you haven't done it.

If you learn to set your own goals and be your own cheerleader your life becomes more interesting. You will set yourself challenges and have a sense of satisfaction that is not dependent on how other people think about what you are doing.

How to get a fresh slant

When you are thinking the same thoughts over and over again you are stuck in a rut. Getting a different perspective on the problem is possible. By changing the way you think about something that is bothering you, you can suddenly realize there are many ways of looking at the same situation. You then have a chance of choosing a different way of dealing with a difficulty. Having analysed the problem you may even decide not to deal with it at all.

Ways to think about a difficulty

When we are struggling with a difficulty we often find ourselves thinking the same thoughts and going over and over the same few pieces of information. The following suggestions will help.

Write down what you are thinking
When you write something down,

- you have the chance to come back to the same thoughts later on and see how they look. You might still feel that what you wrote sums up the situation or you might realize that you have put in too much or you have left something out. You might find that something no longer matters.
- you start to put things into some kind of order. You may write the problem down as a story that starts at the beginning and goes on until now or you might write it down under headings.
- you get the chance to see links and things that keep on happening.
- you could show it to someone else for them to see whether they could make other suggestions.
- you will find it easier to talk about because your ideas won't be so muddled.

If you aren't used to writing something down, a good way to start is with words that pop into your mind. When you look at the words you might see patterns or words that could come together. You could make them into categories. All the words that describe how you feel could be in a category. The timetable of events could be a category. The people involved could be another category.

List your trigger points
Trigger points are when you notice that you have stopped thinking calmly and are beginning to get upset. When you get upset you can over-react. When you over-react you can make an answer more difficult to find. It is worth trying to list your trigger points when you get upset. Sometimes even when reading back over the events you have written down you will notice your feelings changing as you reread certain sections. Each time you notice a change in your reaction you are learning something about yourself.

Think about who else is involved
It is helpful to decide who can and who should be involved in a problem. It is easier if you stop and think before you decide whom to involve. Bear in mind that most of the problems that parents face other parents have dealt with as well. You don't need to hide

away and neither do you need to tell absolutely everybody. It is better to talk to people whom you trust. It is up to you what you do. You will want to talk through things again. Each time you talk to someone you will be learning what works so you might change it next time.

Although many people might have been involved in the incident you and your teenager might be able to sort out the problem together.

Although the problem might seem shocking to you, to other people it is just one of the tricky situations that can happen to teenagers.

Tricky situations – shoplifting

The police brought Jenny home after she had been caught shoplifting. Her best friend had also been picked up by the police and ticked off. Jenny told her parents that there were six other girls, friends of hers at school, who were shoplifting as well but the police hadn't been told about them. Jenny's parents weren't sure whether this was true or not so they thought carefully about how to handle it. They knew what steps they were going to take with Jenny and decided to ring the parents of the other six friends and tell them what Jenny had said. They would also tell them that they weren't convinced she was right but that they were handling the situation at home and they felt the other parents should have the information so they could decide what they wanted to do. Jenny's parents decided not to tell her grandparents or her teachers at school because they didn't need to know if it never happened again.

Consider why you think it is down to you to sort out the problem

As parents we are trained to feel totally responsible for our children. When they are young and vulnerable this training is very important. When little children fall over we rush and pick them up and check they are okay. As children get older we encourage them to pick themselves up, dust themselves down and carry on. It can be hard for parents whose teenagers are getting into trouble or experiencing problems to let the teenagers face it on their own, but it could be the best thing. Think about why you think sorting the problem out is your responsibility. It might be, but then again it might not.

Tricky situations – missing homework

Sam stopped doing her homework. Teachers began to send letters home addressed to her mum and dad asking that they encourage Sam to get her homework done and hand it in. Sam was going to be doing coursework next year. The coursework would count towards her final exam mark and the teachers felt that it was vital that she didn't start to slide now but kept on seeing work done at home as important. Sam's parents agreed with the teachers. They were very upset that Sam seemed to be so dismissive of the advice of her teachers. They sat with Sam and talked to her and tried to get her to understand that they wanted to help her sort out the difficulty. They asked what they could do that would help Sam get her homework done and between them came up with a few ideas. Sam could have a new desk and chair in her room so that it was a more comfortable space in which to do her work. They would get the computer linked up to the Internet so that Sam could do research for her homework on-line.

Sam's parents felt certain that they had turned the situation around and for a few weeks the notes from school stopped. Sam showed them some homework pieces that she had got good marks for and they were relieved.

Unfortunately the situation started to deteriorate again. Once again the letters started coming home and Sam's parents began to worry. This time Sam's parents asked her what help they should give and Sam said she didn't want any help, she just didn't like school. Her parents said they weren't happy with her answer and they were there to help when she wanted to start studying again. They explained that she would have to cope with the detentions or any other consequences of not handing work in. They told her that they would let the school know that they were still concerned about her education but that at the moment Sam had no interest in doing what she was asked to do for homework and they had no way of forcing her to do it. They explained in the letter that they understood the school had some sanctions and they would support the school in any way the school needed.

Help where you can

In a situation like Sam's it is important that teenagers and their parents know what the position is. It is also important that the school knows the real position that the parents are in. Parents are normally the first port of call when there is a difficulty. Whenever something goes wrong parents want and need to be told. Parents don't always have a practical solution to a problem. That doesn't mean they are not interested. It doesn't mean that they wouldn't like to come up with an answer or that they are not horrified that their teenager is not conforming. They can be supportive but they can't sort it out. Parents need to let those in charge of their teenagers know that they don't have a solution. They need to let them know they will support the efforts that are being made to find a way through the difficulty. Adults who are dealing with teenagers will think of more creative ways of dealing with the difficulty when they know parents are supporting them.

Sam continued to avoid doing her homework until she realized if she didn't complete the first half of the Geography coursework she couldn't go on the Geography field trip to Greece.

Think how someone else you know would describe the difficulty

What are all the possible things that somebody might say about your problem? You might imagine their reactions to be:

It's all your fault.
You are never at home.
Lots of teenagers get into scrapes.
You are over-reacting.
It is really serious.
It is temporary.
It is to be expected.
It is funny.

It is easily sorted out.
It is part of growing up.
It is too serious for you to sort out without professional help.

When you look at the difficulty using someone else's point of view, you can shift from a place where you can't think into a place where you can look at options. Having thought about what others could say, you might feel happier about talking through the problem with them. Talking about a difficulty with someone you know gives you the chance to step outside your own reactions and view the predicament from a different standpoint. You don't have to agree with them to benefit from talking to them.

Can you remember when the problem started?

It is rare for problems just to appear without any history to them. It is rare for parents to see the first stages of the difficulty. Teenagers can be, among other things, private, changeable, assertive, argumentative, shy. Even experienced professionals find it difficult, in the early stages of any problem behaviour, to know whether it is going to turn into something more serious or not.

It can help to take out the family photographs and remind yourself of how things were and see if you can recognize when things started to change. Think back through birthday celebrations and Christmases to give you markers and a way of working back to where the problem might have begun. If you find a time where you can tell there was a change think about all the things that were happening in your teenager's life at that time.

It might be:

- the death or illness of a close relative or friend;
- changing school;
- brother or sister leaving home;
- the birth of a baby either in your family or in a close family;
- the loss of a job;
- the breakup of a family;
- an injury;
- an accident.

Can you remember how it started?

This often leads you to see why it started. Sometimes you can remember a change in the way your teenager behaved. It may have been a change in how he spoke to you, ate, and got on with other people in the family or how he felt about school.

What do you think will happen if the problem doesn't get sorted out?

It is worth thinking about what will happen if there isn't a solution. If you think about it before you react you will be able to decide on the seriousness of the problem and the steps you need to take. You don't always have to go 'gung ho' to find a solution to a problem. The problem might get itself sorted out. Someone else might sort it out or your teenager will mature and the problem will be history.

Think about who wants the difficulty to be sorted out?

Do you think this is a real problem or is the problem that other people are putting pressure on you to react as if it is a problem. Stop and think about who has been talking to you about the problem and what they have been saying. Clarity is a great protector. Knowing clearly where you stand will help you to avoid over-reacting. The world isn't a perfect place and every individual in it has a weakness in some area. You might be able to live with your teenager's untidiness because you know he does change the sheets regularly. Your daughter may find his untidiness outrageous but that is her problem.

Is there anyone who doesn't want the problem to be sorted out?

It is not uncommon for one parent to see something as an over-whelming difficulty while the other one sees it as a temporary hiccup. Just stop and think about how other adults have responded to your concerns. Don't expect everyone to endorse all your decisions. Know your own ground and why you are doing what you are doing. You don't have to be right all the time. You are learning as well.

Has it happened before?

What did you do then? Is this time different? How is it different?

All these questions give you a framework for thinking about what you already know. Sometimes a problem arises in a new situation and you think it is a new problem. When you think it through you might realize that the problem isn't new at all and in fact you have lots of ways of coping with it.

What do you think you need to sort out the problem?

List the things you think you need to solve the problem. They could be more confidence, support from a partner, less to do, a week's holiday, more knowledge. As you list what you need you see the detail of the problem. You also begin to think about what you want those things for. If you write down that you need more support from your partner because then you would have some time to talk to your teenager you begin to see the moves you can make.

Who do you think you need to help you sort out the problem?

By listing the people you want to help you you begin to untangle the problem. The more you are untangling the problem the easier it will be to ask one of the people on the list for help and the clearer the explanation will be of why you need the help and what help you would like.

Why do you think you can't sort out the problem?

You might think you can't do anything about a problem because you think you don't have enough skills. Being faced by a problem can make you forget all the skills you do have. By writing down what is stopping you from sorting it out you will break down your sense of powerlessness. It will be obvious to you that in many other situations in your life you do have the skills to sort out difficulties. You will remind yourself that you are not a weak person in every situation in your life.

Do you want someone else to change?

Sometimes there can be a problem in your life that has nothing to do with the difficulty your teenager is having. Sometimes we use every difficulty that comes our way as evidence that if this major problem were sorted out everything else would be all right as well.

Tricky situations – I should never have said yes

Kieran's dad did freelance work at home so that he could look after the children. Kieran's mum had to work in town, which meant leaving quite early and often getting back late. As her career took off and it became obvious she couldn't follow her career and take her share in the day-to-day family responsibilities it was decided that Kieran's father would cut down on his workload so that he had the time to sort things out.

Whenever there was a problem with the children Kieran's dad felt that the arrangement was not working. Instead of trying to sort the problems out he brooded on his situation. He didn't feel he could tell his partner because it might sound as if he was putting pressure on her to stop working so hard at her career. He didn't feel it was in his power to solve the problems. He felt every problem was because of the situation he had agreed to. The children's problems mounted up. It felt that home was no longer a place of rest for anybody.

Because Kieran's dad believed that he couldn't say anything to his partner he just went round and round in circles. He never broke the problem down into manageable pieces and never spotted anything he could do something about. He never asked for help.

Do you think you could work out a small way to change what you do?

Difficulties may diminish or disappear altogether if you are able to identify the small changes you can make. Small changes feel possible. If there is a difficulty and you think you need to make a huge change then the problem may not be tackled because a huge change can feel too hard to manage.

Tricky situations – temper, temper

Sophie would always flare up in the same way and for the same reasons. She knew that she had a temper and if she tried to sort anything out while she was feeling angry she would just make matters worse. She could explain to her teenagers that when she got cross she needed some time to be cross and deal with her crossness on her own. She would leave the house and go for a walk while she fumed. When she got back she would be able to deal with any difficulty in a rational way. She still flared up but she gave herself an opportunity to cool down.

Bev was aware that she had a temper. She would explode if the music were too loud, dirty cups were left unwashed in the sink or if she got a note from school. She felt that the only people who were able to sort out difficulties in a mature way were people who could control their tempers. Since she could not control her temper she felt she could not sort out any difficulties. She was stuck.

Did you think you would never have this problem?

If you clarify how you used to think about a problem before it happened to you you can let ignorant and innocent thoughts belong to the past.

All of us can fall into the trap of believing some things will never happen to us. We are ignorant and innocent until we experience for ourselves something that we had only thought about. By acknowledging that the thoughts you had before were based on hearsay and probably quite shallow you can deal with what is in front of you. You will stop worrying about what you used to think.

What used you to think about people who had this problem?

It can be a nightmare for people whose professional life is dealing with teenagers to find their own children have teenage problems just like their teenage clients. Just like the parents of their clients they are no better at handling their own children's problems than the people who come to them for advice. In the same way that doctors are advised not to treat their own families because they are too involved, professionals who work with families should seek advice, if they need it, when dealing with their own families. Professionals are always reminding their clients that no one is perfect. They may need an outsider to remind them that they too are human.

Do you know anyone else who has had this difficulty?

Often when faced with a problem we forget all that we have heard. Try to recall whether you have heard of anyone else being in a similar situation. If you can bring someone to mind, do you know what that person did, or is there someone you can ask about the course of action they took? Finding out how someone else coped doesn't mean that you have to follow their actions exactly but it will mean you might get some fresh ideas or some reassurance that you are not on your own. Help-lines can give suggested outlines of what to do or who to contact.

What sort of person do you think you are when things go wrong and something needs to change?

Do you think you:

Concede– admit defeat?
If you concede you give up your responsibility for finding a solution. You let someone else sort it out.

Correct – set right, amend?
If you correct the situation you try and find ways of reallocating responsibilities so that everything can still happen, the homework can still be done, the teenager can still have friends.

Control – have the power to direct?
If you control the situation you impose your will on the event and on those involved. You decide what will be done and what people will have to do.

Cope – deal with the situation competently?
If you cope you make sure you are always available for whatever happens and do whatever has been decided. You are at everybody's

beck and call. You make few demands.

Compromise – settle the dispute by mutual concession?

If you compromise you ask everyone to say what he or she can offer to solve the problem. You then find some way of everyone getting a bit of what they need.

Compel – force someone to do it?

If you compel you can only operate in certain situations by using force whether that is physical, psychological or emotional.

Collapse – lose courage?

If you collapse when there is a problem you feel that you are worth nothing. You feel you can't possibly deal with the situation in a rational manner. The feeling overwhelms you.

The reality is that most of the time you will react in a combination of ways. It is worth knowing which reaction you have at different times. Self-knowledge means that you have the information if you want to change.

3

Nurturing me, nurturing you

Bounce back from the body blows

You can feel devastated by the things your teenagers do or say.

It is essential that you don't let your own self-esteem be undermined by this teenage behaviour.

It is unrealistic to think that your teenager will worry about how you will feel when they are horrible. Even if they do have a fleeting thought that you might be upset about what they are going to do, it will only be fleeting. Teenagers often do just what they want regardless of what you have said.

Remember:

- You are able to do many things.
- You do have friends.
- Most people treat you with respect.
- You have good ideas.
- You can get on with your own life.
- You can have your own standards.
- You have ways of protecting yourself.

Freedom not licence

When Sarah found that her two sons were inviting their friends round to the house to smoke dope she felt let down. She felt that all her friends would think she was a mother who didn't care what her sons got up to or what her house was used for. She didn't hesitate. She rang the parents of the boys who had been coming round to the house to tell them that she had never given permission or condoned in any way what was going on. The parents all spoke to their sons and the problem stopped immediately.

Sarah had always had an open house policy for all her children. She enjoyed the activity and hearing how young people saw the world. As the youngsters got older they misread the freedom they had been given. They didn't realize that Sarah had standards for the way her house could be used. Once it was made clear, the situation settled down. Young people still came round and they respected Sarah's standards. Although Sarah had been shocked by what had happened she took positive action based on her position as a parent and a householder.

You are entitled to your standards

When your children were young you had spoken and unspoken house rules. You expected them to be kept. The same thing applies when your children are older. Your hospitality does not have to be exploited. If you make rules you can give your teenagers some protection when one of their friends goes too far.

You do not have to compromise

Parents who stay calm through the sometimes tempestuous times of living with teenagers know how to give themselves space and time to consider how to protect their own standards. They work out how they want to act and how they want others to act towards them. They work out what they want to say and how they want to say it.

Mull it over

Parents can easily feel unbalanced when their teenagers demand immediate answers and instantaneous decisions. Teenagers can often push parents into feeling destabilized by harassing them into giving quick decisions. Don't be afraid to take time to consider what you want to do. We can all think of times when mulling something over or talking it through with a friend meant we came up with an idea for handling a situation in a sensible way.

Ask for space and time to think

If you say you will give your teenager a response later, tell them when later will be. That way you can cut out the constant hassling for an answer. If they insist they need a response sooner than that, you decide whether you are prepared to compromise.

Dealing with a fait accompli

A fait accompli is defined as a thing that has already been done and is not reversible. A parent may state categorically that their teenager is not to do something. The teenager however thinks the parent's rule is unfair, inconsequential, odd or wrong and so ignores what the parent has said.

You need to see a fait accompli for what it is. It is someone making a decision without any consideration of your desires. If you see it this way then their disregard for your wishes means that you are at liberty to decide whether or not you will help and if you do help, how much you will help.

Marcus had been told not to go to his friend's during the week because there was no adult there and in the past the boys had helped themselves to some cans of lager and spent hours and hours playing computer games. That left Marcus hyperactive, unable to sleep and impossible to get up in the morning for school. Marcus was allowed to do other things in the evening and often met his mates to practise skateboarding.

When he bounced in late one evening it was obvious that he had been to his friend's house. His parents made no comment. In the morning he was still asleep when it was time for them to leave for work. His parents went off to their jobs. Half an hour after getting to work Marcus' mother got a worried phone call from him. He said he was going to be in awful trouble for missing a test at school so would she please phone the school to say that he was not well. She said no.

Teenagers need to know that when they decide to do what they want to do other people can decide the position they will take as well.

Dealing with the inevitable

As your children become teenagers and become more independent things change. When your children were growing up you invested money, time, interest and emotions. You were making a family. You were creating a home. You were providing support. You were doing all of this in hundreds of practical ways and your children appreciated most of them.

You had to learn how necessary you were when your children were tiny and dependent. Now they are teenagers you have to learn to cope with the change as they find their own ways to earn money, spend their time, develop their interests and make new relationships.

Feeling unsettled by change is normal. Feeling upset and abandoned is natural. It doesn't matter how much you prepare for these changes and think you will be able to deal with them, it is not until they happen that you realize what they mean.

Who wants a piece of cake?

Mary made a chocolate cake that all her family loved. It had become the treat of choice for celebrations, cheering up and a reward for effort. When Tom had a lovely school report Mary made a chocolate cake. When Roisin fell off her bike and had to have stitches there was chocolate cake. When they came back from Grandad's funeral there was chocolate cake. The chocolate cake affirmed everybody's connection to the family.

Mary felt particularly confident because she was the one who had created that family experience for everyone else. It was one of those 'I know how to be a mother' experiences. What Mary hadn't realized was that being a mother in that way may not last. When Tom had a row with his dad over a scratch that had appeared on the car Mary made a chocolate cake. She expected that as usual the cake would serve to, 'pour oil on troubled waters'. In the past, the arrival of a chocolate cake had meant that everyone made friends again.

When Mary brought the chocolate cake in, Tom and his dad were talking without anger. She put the cake down. They kept on talking as she cut the cake. When Mary offered some to Tom he said very nicely that he didn't want any. Mary was horrified. One of the certainties of her life as a mother, a peacemaker and a lynchpin of the family had been shaken. It had been shaken just a little but enough to make Mary wonder what her next move was supposed to be.

Not every tradition lasts for ever

One of the traps that we can fall into is to think that the family we have made will last for ever in the way we made it. We can fool ourselves into thinking that because we, along with our children, enjoy doing something when they are seven they will want to do the same thing at seventeen.

For some families eating a Sunday meal together becomes a tradition while the children are young. The ritual looks so firmly established it could never change. It serves so many purposes and fulfills so many needs.

- It is a steadying influence in the week.
- It is the chance for everyone to sit down at the same time.
- Everybody loves the food.
- It is a chance for conversation.
- It is a meal with protected time.
- It is familiar.
- It is a tradition.
- It feels grown up.

For other families other times are full of meaning. They may watch a football match, go shopping, go to church, or weekends away. What makes these times or events so significant is that there is an emotional bond between everybody who is involved. It seems to be so permanent and so secure. As children reach their teenage years what was true can become a myth. They are happy to look back on it. They are glad that it happened but they don't feel the need for it now. What seemed so secure and unchanging and reliable starts to shift.

Because the changes are gradual, parents often can't prepare themselves to cope with the sense of loss when those special events stop being so special to everyone in the family. Family traditions seem so secure when they are not buffeted by change. When they do change, even slightly, that change can undermine everybody's confidence in what seemed to be an emblem of family unity. It seemed to be proof that each member of the family was safe and secure within the family.

The undermining of family traditions can be all the more shocking because it can happen at any time and without any warning.

Parental responsibilities – can two minds think as one?

What is the likelihood of two adults agreeing on every aspect of their lives together?

You might think that hanging a coat up is quite a reasonable thing to expect people to do but your partner thinks that it is an invasion of his liberty. Your partner might want silence before eight o'clock in the morning while you want to start the day with radios on in every room in the house.

You might think playing Elton John CDs by candlelight is the ideal way to relax while she thinks the only way to switch off is to watch reruns of *Star Trek*.

What is the likelihood of two adults agreeing on every aspect of their parental responsibilities? You might think a curfew of eleven o'clock is quite late enough for your teenagers to be out. Your partner might think twelve o'clock is fine and be happy to go and pick them up. You might think they should get used to travelling by bus, while she thinks it's okay for them to have a scooter.

Compromise or agree to differ

Compromises can take different forms.

- Both parents may accept that something mustn't be done at all because one parent thinks that it is wrong.
- Both parents may accept that something will be done because one parent thinks that it is right.
- Both parents accept that whichever parent is at home has the choice. One parent may think that the dishes can be left until there are no more to be used and then a big washing-up session happens. The other partner might think that the washing-up should be done after each meal, that way they stay on top of things. When one person is away from home the person that remains has it their way.

Often parents don't agree with each other's ideas. This does not need to be a problem because teenagers need to learn to accept differences in what people will tolerate. They may try and play one adult off against the other but there is no reason why parents and their friends should be manipulated in this way.

If parents have different views on anything to do with their joint responsibilities they need to find a way of dealing with it. If they don't find a way they risk allowing the teenager to undermine them. It is often appropriate and necessary for the parents to be taking the adult role. As teenagers grow up, the times and places where their parents take the adult role shift and change.

Nobody ever sees it my way

Sometimes you may not be in a relationship where you can compromise. You will feel as if you are being overridden. Your wishes will be ignored and your ideas scorned or discounted. The danger of being in a position like this is that you begin to see yourself as worthless. You may be fine at work or with friends but the minute you are with your family you feel trapped and insignificant.

Escape routes you can use when you feel trapped by your family

It is important to value yourself. It is possible to value yourself. It is your responsibility to value yourself.

You will feel happier with yourself if you:

- work out ways to change how you react;
- find ways of giving yourself space before you have to react;
- find ways of getting support – it could be reading a book or talking to a friend;
- recognize any changes no matter how small;
- don't put a time limit on feeling better.

You can use any or all of these steps to help you regain your self-respect, self-worth and confidence in who you are:

Take one step at a time
This may appear to be an overused cliché. The reason it is a key piece of advice for many self-help programmes is that it encourages you to take the first step rather than feel powerless. It also encourages you to realize that this is only one step on the way. This helps you be more realistic about the time it takes to change. If you take one step you may then see that because you have moved from one position there are several courses of action you could take.

Feel enthusiastic and positive about the steps you are going to take
If you don't feel any enthusiasm you will build in failure and certainly take out any enjoyment. Having enthusism for something means that you have a strong interest in it. Having a strong interest means that you will override the negative. It doesn't mean that you will be reckless but it means that you will seize opportunities as they happen and stay interested when there are no opportunities.

Take a step that you can take
If you decide on a step to take that is actually impossible for you to make at the time, it will not help you. If you don't recognize that

your decision was wrong you may feel even more inadequate and powerless. If the step that you choose is within what you can do, real change will happen even if it only appears to be quite small.

Know your step may be different from everybody else's step
The important thing about making a change for yourself is that you see yourself as an individual. You are not going to take the same steps as someone else because you are not exactly the same as them. You can tailor your own steps to what you need and what you can do. Devising your own steps encourages you to take responsibility for yourself and the changes you are trying to make.

Know that you can see whether your step is working
Don't be dependent on the views of other people about whether you are getting it right or not. As you become more confident you will also become more discerning about differences that you can notice. You might notice how your feelings have changed or how much longer you can think about something without getting upset or giving up. You might notice how much faster you are at thinking what you want or how much clearer your explanations of what you need have become.

Know that you can be flexible
Once you start to change things for yourself you learn how to think, how to listen and how to discriminate when a situation which is challenging arises. You will feel confident that some solution can be found. You won't feel bound by what has happened before or locked into behaving in a way that is expected if that is not going to work.

Know that you can be creative
If you don't expect to come up with solutions to problems immediately you will be able to be still and consider what you know. Your mind will be open and alert. As you consider what is happening you will be able to see the problem from different perspectives. By getting a wider view of a difficulty you can often devise creative solutions.

Know what you want to do

When you feel responsible for sorting a problem out you can feel that until the problem is solved you can't relax. You think you shouldn't allow in any other thoughts that would distract you from thinking about the problem. You can take a break if you want to. It may even help.

Look back at what you have achieved with a sense of pride

It doesn't matter how small the step is or how easily you thought it was to do, you must recognize the progress you have made. The fact that you have made progress is something to be proud of. You will stop yourself making progress if you dismiss every achievement as unimportant. If you were aiming to change something, and when you have succeeded you only look at what still needs to be done, you are changing the goal posts. You will feel frustrated at your apparent lack of capability. You have made yourself look as though you can't be successful.

Joan despaired of ever being able to keep her kitchen like her friends'. They seemed to be able to put things away, know where they had put things and find a clean tea towel whenever they needed it. No matter how much time Joan spent in the kitchen trying to get it shipshape it never worked. She still ended up with muddled up cupboards, cluttered surfaces and piles of dirty tea towels. She decided to take one step at a time. She would aim to have a clean tea towel whenever she needed it. Her first step was to buy a pack of six new tea towels. This solved the problem. Instead of feeling pleased with her progress towards her goal, however, she felt despondent about the muddled-up cupboards and depressed about the cluttered work surfaces. She gave up bothering.

If Joan had felt proud of what she had achieved already with her first step she would have felt she was competent enough to sort out the next bit.

See yourself as a competent, capable and confident individual

A competent person recognizes what they don't know or what is outside their capabilities in each situation.

If you are competent, capable and confident you won't trivialize the efforts of others or your own efforts. You will understand the efforts that have been made and appreciate the time that has been put in. If you trivialize what someone else is doing they will stop helping. They will feel their efforts are so insignificant to you that it doesn't matter to you whether they do it or not. If you trivialize your own efforts you will give up because you won't see what you do as important or worthwhile.

When you see things as complicated but possible you give yourself a chance. If you see things as complicated and impossible you throw away your chances. You frighten yourself away from having a go at working out how to do it. You scare yourself off asking somebody else to help you.

Feel determined about what you are going to do next

You can feel nervous and still be determined. You can think something is hard but still be determined to do it.

Friends in need – helping a friend to regain their balance

All parents hope that the teenage years will be the time when the children they have needed to care for quite intimately in their younger years work out how to lead their own lives. They hope they will be busy, involved, interesting and pleasant to be with. For most parents there will be times when their dream seems to be taking shape to some extent.

For some parents the teenage years do not run as smoothly. For some parents the teenage years are a nightmare.

Most parents are pleased and relieved when their own teenagers are doing all right. It can be hard thinking of what to say if your friends have teenagers who are having difficulties. On any day, parents of teenagers could be:

- taking them to an exam;
- taking them to court;
- taking them to hospital;
- taking them to see the head teacher;
- taking them to a party.

If you want to support a friend who is facing difficult times with their teenager you can be there to listen.

For one friend a difficult time could be when their teenage daughter discovers she is pregnant. For another friend it could be deeply distressing when their teenager does not pass the auditions for the orchestra that everyone assumed they would join as soon as they were old enough. For another friend it could be their teenager coming in late and always drunk.

Before you offer yourself as a listener remember that you will need to avoid making comparisons between your teenager and your friend's teenager. Comparisons are rarely helpful and in this situation unlikely to be helpful. This listening time is for the other parent to talk about what they want.

Your friend, out of politeness, may ask you about your teenagers, so keep your answers short and as low key as possible. The purpose of your visit is to give them a chance to talk about what has happened in their family, and although it may be far more comfortable for you to talk about what has happened to your family lately that is not why you are there.

Many people shy away when someone they know has a problem because they are not too sure how to handle it. They worry that:

- they might call at an awkward time;
- they might make their friend feel worse;
- they might not be able to come up with any good ideas;
- they might not know enough;
- they are not the best person.

Remember – whenever somebody is reeling from a trauma they will always be comforted if you can show that you care. It reminds them that this problem is a part of their life, not their whole life.

There are people out there who are thinking about them and sympathizing.

When you speak to your friend you can lift their spirit enormously by telling them that you think they are doing well. This may seem a silly thing to say when somebody is deeply distressed but when you feel as if you are not coping it is comforting to know that someone else can see the effort you are making. When people feel as though they are not coping, a little encouragement can go a long way.

Things you can offer to do

- Make a phone call on their behalf or help them plan what they are going to say if they make the call.
- Go with them to a meeting or an appointment. You could be the driver and/or a supporter in the meeting. When people have difficult meetings to face about their teenagers, having a friend there to take notes can give them some way of checking what was said.
- Find out some information for your friend that might help. Be careful how you use the information. It may be better to read it yourself before passing it on to your friend. You might decide not to pass it on immediately but to pass it on when the time seems right.
- Talk to the teenager yourself.
- Find someone else who might be able to help the teenager.

Remember that you are a guest and you must honour the privacy of the family. No matter how tempted you are to mention what is going on when you are speaking to other friends, avoid the temptation. Think how you would feel if someone passed on private information without your permission.

If you suddenly have a bright idea of what to do next ring your friend and check whether it is okay for you to pursue it.

No matter how uncomfortable it feels to help a friend, or how worried you feel that the help you have given isn't quite right, sincere help is appreciated.

4

Crisis, what crisis?

Crisis management

To stay mentally healthy in a crisis you have to make sure that you look after yourself.

Don't try to:

- live someone else's life;
- cover up for someone else's mistakes;
- take on someone else's responsibilities;
- cope with more than you can handle.

Don't think that:

- the only way to show your concern is to look miserable and stressed;
- the only way to support others is to defend them;
- you have to accept what is being given.

Do:

- focus on the things you can do;
- allow other people to do what they can do;
- make it clear where you stand.

When teenagers live dangerously

Helen was a lively baby. She seemed to have no sense of danger. At the park she would swing higher, climb further and delight in spinning very fast on the merry-go-round. She was great fun to be with. She seemed to bubble with life.

When her father started working away Helen found it difficult to cope. She began to take risks. By the time she was twelve her parents were at their wits' end. Helen was no longer interested in school. She was choosing friends that her parents felt were unsuitable and she was defiant. Both of Helen's parents tried to reason with her. They couldn't believe that they had a child whom they felt was in such danger but who was not interested in anything they had to say. They tried everything to get her to behave like a more reasonable and responsible teenager but they were powerless. She was doing all the things parents of teenagers hope they won't do.

The only thing that Helen's parents found they could try to do was to remain as calm as possible.

Until Helen was twenty-one she lived a precarious life. At twenty-one she scared herself when she ended up in hospital. Although this had happened before, for some reason this time the scare gave Helen the impetus to think about the direction in which her life was heading and make some changes. Gradually she sorted out each detail. She stopped taking drugs, she enrolled on a course and she began to make friends with people who were trying to make something out of their lives. The improvements continued.

How Helen's parents coped through Helen's dark days

Helen's mother enrolled on a course in order to have something else to think about and a positive goal in the midst of the misery. She felt a failure as a mother but she knew that she would stand by her daughter and help whenever there seemed to be something she could do.

Helen's father was devastated. For a time he became a bitter and disillusioned man. He adored his daughter and couldn't cope with what she was doing to herself. He had no idea what he should do so he decided to take the lead from his wife. Supporting her meant that he had shifted his responsibility from trying to sort out Helen's problem to being there as a help for her mother. This was something he could manage.

How Helen's parents coped with their social life

While Helen had been in her dark days Helen's mother and father had to listen to the implied and direct criticism from their friends about how they were handling Helen and the choices they were making or the reactions they were having. They had to listen to their daughter being described as a stereotype rather than as a person. They had to listen to their friends gossip to each other about Helen's latest disasters. Their friends had teenagers who passed exams and thought about what to do in the year between school and university. Even though Helen's parents were horrified and in despair their lives still continued. They went to work, went for walks, had holidays, all the things their friends were doing. It was like a surreal world.

How Helen's parents took a step back

They were always there for all their children, including Helen. They decided that Helen should take the consequences for any of her actions but they were there. They didn't protect her but they showed Helen that she was still their daughter. They gave time to their other children.

How Helen's parents showed they cared

Helen's parents were never really sure what they should be doing but they felt it was important that Helen and everyone else knew that they were parents who were ready to help. Even when their hearts were breaking they kept remembering that Helen was their child. They just held on to their position as her parents. They didn't try to intercede when things went wrong. That would have been pointless. They didn't make promises on her behalf because they knew they had no guarantee Helen would keep them. If any promises were made about Helen changing then they would have to be made by Helen.

How Helen's parents kept their heads above water

Financially, life was difficult because for many years Helen stole from members of the family whenever she could.

Emotionally, life with Helen was exhausting because she would try to use up every emotional resource her parents had. They kept reminding themselves that they had done their best and were continuing to do their best.

For them, as for so many parents, the nightmare had an end.

How Helen's parents helped her to reach adulthood

There were many times in her teenage years where they were terrified for her safety. There were many times when they wanted to blame each other, society or her friends for the misery that they were feeling, but they tried not to. They managed to keep in their minds that Helen was choosing to lead this life and Helen would have to take the consequences. Those consequences had an effect on members of her family but they too could make choices.

How Helen's parents kept themselves going

The family members tried to make positive choices in the short term, medium term and long term. In the short term they might plan a nice day out. In the medium term they might make plans to redesign the garden. In the long term they made decisions about their careers. No matter what Helen was doing they still had lives that were moving forward.

Ways to help yourself cope in a crisis

- Try not to criticize anyone, especially yourself. Criticism is a waste of time and energy. In a crisis you need all the time and energy you can get to find positive courses of action.
- Remind yourself of the good times.
- Make some time for yourself.

When teenagers live daringly

Not all the dangers that teenagers expose themselves to or flirt with are as life threatening as those Helen was involved in. However, for a parent minor problems caused by the choices that their teenagers are making can be very worrying. To the teenager it may seem no big deal to get a tattoo. To the parents who know that a choice you make when you are a teenager may leave you with a reputation that you don't want as an adult it can be far more serious. Parents can feel very concerned that their teenager may be unwittingly throwing away future opportunities.

David was really into heavy metal music. He spent hours practising two chords on his bass guitar. He wore black tee shirts decorated with frightening and horrible images. His hair hung over his face in an unwashed curtain cutting him off from those around him. He painted his room purple with black doors. He slashed his curtains into what he said were artistic representations of burial shrouds. His parents tried to explain what other people would think when they saw the way David was choosing to express himself. David said that was their problem and other people didn't see things in the same narrow and prejudiced way that his parents did.

David's friends were all similar to David, seeming to delight in toying with the world of the occult, images of death and destruction and devising music lyrics that appeared written to cause the most offence possible.

When David and his friends heard that a favourite band was coming to play at the local university there was great excitement. Someone knew someone else who could get them the tickets and this would be the cultural highlight of their year. The concert was fantastic. David said it was well worth the money and he and his mates, when they passed their driving tests, would be able to travel to other cities to watch the band again. The group of friends who had been to the concert together arranged to meet up later in the week to relive the highlights of Saturday and the band. Walking through town to meet the others one of David's friends was spotted by a group of teenagers who took offence at the tee shirt he was wearing. The gang chased David's mate, finally tripping him up and pushing him around. He was quite battered and very upset by the incident. By the time he got to David and the others he was shaking and close to tears.

When David got home he told his parents what had happened. They were concerned for his friend and listened to what David knew about what had taken place. David wanted to talk and they felt they should listen. They were relieved that David was taking what had happened to his friend so seriously. They hoped he would remember the things they had said about other people and the way they would make assumptions about him because of the image he and his friends were choosing to give to the world.

What you say does matter

When things go wrong children often come back to talk to their parents. They need someone they can trust, who cares about them and will listen to them while they are putting the bits of the jigsaw of their life together and trying to make sense of the world.

For David, a few more pieces had been put in the jigsaw. He could see that, whether it was right or wrong, people you didn't know would make assumptions based on the way you looked. He could begin to work out how he could keep himself safe while still enjoying what he wanted to do.

It's up to you

Part of growing up is deciding which risks you will take and which ones are not worth doing or are too dangerous.

Part of growing up is finding out how far you are prepared to go to follow your beliefs or interests. You start to see that the protection you had when you were a child, the freedom to say what you thought and do what you liked, was actually provided by adults. As you grow up people will ask you to justify your ideas, prove your intentions and show that you are as good as you say you are.

There are other people out there

It is helpful if parents can gently point out that while it may be wrong for people to make assumptions based on looks, lifestyle and opinions, that is what happens. You can agree with your teenagers that this is unfair but you can point out that:

- There are other ways of getting your point over if that is really what you want to do.
- You do not have to convince everyone around you to think the way you think.
- You can be loyal and true to your ideas and principles without ramming them down everybody's throat.
- Letting other people have their opinions does not mean you have betrayed yours.
- Finding ways to talk about your interests is just as useful as finding ways to listen to other people talk about theirs.
- People don't automatically dislike you simply because you hold a different opinion to theirs.
- At the same time as you are developing your opinions you need to find ways to manage the effects that those opinions have on you and on other people.

Anger management

Most teenagers get angry. Most parents of teenagers get angry too.

Anger can come when children become teenagers because teenagers feel they can make rules. Anger can come when teenagers feel that their rights and freedoms are being challenged or jeopardized.

Parents can feel that their freedom to live in a house where they make the rules is in jeopardy when they are living with teenagers. Teenagers can feel that their right to live in a house in the way they want, and being true to the way they want to be, is not being allowed.

Different strokes for different folks

Some people are happy to get angry. They think that getting things off their chest is the best way of getting over them.

Some families are happy if every member of the family expresses their anger. Family arguments, shouting matches, tears and slammed doors are part of the way that they deal with each other. The fundamental relationships are strong, although to the outside world it can look alarming.

In other families any display of anger is seen as threatening. The members of the family expect to find ways of dealing with their frustration, upset or displeasure alone.

Many families can cope with some anger as long as it doesn't take over. The occasional outburst is seen as a way of letting people know that there is a problem that needs sorting out. There is no right or wrong, only preference. Even within families there can be individuals who are happy to argue, scream and shout while others would prefer to deal with the upset quietly.

If you can think rationally at the same time as you feel upset you will be able to resolve problems that arise relatively quickly. The hardest arguments to be rational about are the ones that you are involved in.

Learning to think rationally

Thinking rationally means that you are working out how to get things in proportion. The word rational comes from the word ratio which means how one thing weighs or measures against another. We feel irrational when our response is out of proportion to the problem. We feel others are being irrational when their response is not in the proportion we expect.

In families, how much one thing matters to one person is often in conflict with how much it matters to someone else.

How to avoid conflict

Parents or someone has to try and explain:

- Why one person thinks one way and another feels quite differently.
- How both people have good reason for believing what they think is right.
- How people can live together even when they believe different things.
- How important it is for families to find some way of living together as calmly as possible.

Not every family feels that calm is necessary. They believe everyone should fight their corner. They believe everyone has to work out on their own how to cope with other members of the family.

It matters to me

When Tony came storming out of his bedroom ready to punch his little brother his dad grabbed him and told him to calm down. Tony was shaking with fury and close to tears because his brother had gone into his room. His dad asked what his brother had done in his room. Tony said he hadn't done anything but that wasn't the point.

Tony, like other teenagers, felt his room should be private because:

- it was the only place in the world he could call his own;
- it was somewhere where he could make the rules;
- he had secret things that he didn't want to run the risk of anyone else seeing;
- it was where he was growing up;
- it was away from the public gaze;
- he had been told it was his private space.

Tony was happy for other people to go into his room but only by invitation and only to do what had been agreed.

Tony's brother had threatened Tony's right to privacy and therefore Tony felt entitled to be really angry.

My place, my space

When people go into a teenager's room, without an invitation, it can feel to the teenager that they are implying that he or she:

- shouldn't have a space that they can call their own;
- doesn't have the right to make the rules anywhere;
- shouldn't have secrets;
- does not need any privacy;
- shouldn't object to them or anything that they want to do.

The person who goes into the teenager's room might feel that they are justified because:

- they were picking up the washing;
- they own the house;
- they wanted to see what was what;
- they wanted to borrow something;
- they were putting something back.

This is why sometimes teenagers' reactions can seem to be irrational. A younger brother goes in to a bedroom just to see what is there. An older brother feels that all his needs for a secure space of his own are being trashed.

Shared boundaries

Teenagers who have to share a room often work out very strict boundaries. Setting boundaries in a shared space allows the occupants to develop individually within that space. They work out that one person's ideas about tidiness or timings don't have to affect them. Headphones can allow each person to listen to their own music. Curtains can screen off light.

Those sharing can be rational each time there is a conflict and it is worked out.

Getting things back in proportion

When there is an outburst that seems irrational parents can feel very alarmed by such an over-the-top reaction. While it is important to diffuse the over-the-top reaction it is also important to go through what caused the problem.

Sometimes when there has been an outburst in the family you have to try and work out why things have got out of proportion. You might need to explain one person's point of view to someone else or you might need someone else to explain his or her point of view to you.

Sometimes you won't get to the bottom of the outburst because what you need to know is being kept secret on purpose. Sometimes you won't get to the bottom of the outburst because the other person won't know why they have been upset either.

Respecting boundaries

It is easy to forget that privacy matters to everybody. One of the problems of parenthood is that your right to privacy seems to disappear for years. You have to remind yourself of what it was like when you were a teenager wanting your space so you can protect the right of your teenagers to the boundaries they have set.

When teenagers live uncaringly

You can feel devastated if your teenager seems to be abandoning all the values and training you have worked so hard to provide.

When Joel was in junior school his mum and dad were very proud of him and he seemed pleased to make them proud. He wasn't a perfect child but they didn't want perfection. He was delighted to share his successes with them. He joined in when they were having company, when they were working in the garden and when they went on walks. He was loving and respectful when things went wrong.

His parents felt very confident that they had a good relationship with Joel and were pretty confident that the teenage years would pose no problem. They felt that the way they had brought Joel up would mean that their friendship with him would be secure. It seemed they had built up such a firm foundation.

When Joel was eleven all his parents thoughts about their son started being challenged. Joel appeared to turn into a different person. His parents began to feel as though they were living with a stranger. It wasn't that Joel took drugs or rebelled in a dramatic way, it was more a descent into a sloppy and rude way of doing everything, from eating his meals to speaking to his grandparents when they came to visit.

At first Joel's parents felt that they could remind him of the way they wanted him to behave – that somehow or other it had just slipped his mind to be reasonable. Gradually they realized that he was choosing to behave that way and was determined to defend his right to behave that way.

Even irritating teenagers need their parents

Parents can feel despairing when their teenagers behave in an embarrassing or irritating way because they feel:

- their values have been rejected;
- their teenagers have nothing to do with them;
- they are still expected to sort out the problems but they don't know how;
- they have lost the relationship they had when their children were young.

What Joel's parents did to support Joel

Joel's parents realized he was not going to do what they asked or listen to what they had to say. In order to cope they decided to:

- ignore his behaviour with his grandparents. They did discuss the problem with the grandparents and explained that while they did not approve or feel happy about the way Joel was behaving they felt this was the best tactic. The grandparents understood and dealt with Joel in their own manner.
- leave Joel behind when they went out for meals. Joel was told that when he ate politely then he would be invited to go with them.

Teenagers are still children. They really are very dependent on their parents for instructions, advice and for their self-esteem. Joel's parents continued to take their role seriously by deciding on what they would accept and what they needn't accept. They needn't accept that they had to take a son out who would show them up in public. They, together with his grandparents, could manage a phase of uncaring behaviour.

5

How to like teenagers even when they drive you mad

Teenagers aren't another species, although sometimes it feels as though they are. Sometimes living with teenagers can try the patience of a saint, let alone the average parent. But remember that most teenagers, when they get the chance to show that they care about the environment, other people and their friends, come up trumps.

It's not the end of the world

We all know people who spend their lives noticing what isn't there, whether it is a missing slice of lemon in a gin and tonic or a space to sit down in a favourite café. They don't handle these blips calmly. Instead they respond extremely negatively and with the same force as should perhaps be reserved for something that has real importance. We may even be a bit like that ourselves. Teenagers are people too and some of them will be irritated when the tiniest thing goes wrong.

Take the rough with the smooth

Probably all of us can remember a time when we reduced at least one parent to tears by being dissatisfied with what we had or what was happening. We may pretend to ourselves that we were easy to live with, grateful for what we had and appreciative of all that our parents did for us. However, if we are being honest we know that there were plenty of times when we were ungrateful, unkind and unappreciative.

We were sometimes mean to our parents.

Why do teenagers seem to be mean?

Sometimes teenagers seem to be mean on purpose and sometimes seem to be mean by accident. The truth is that teenagers are at the mercy of a whole host of emotions. These emotions are powerful and all-consuming.

Sometimes they want to let you know they are unhappy with you and, because they feel they have no real power, they exaggerate what they are doing or saying to make sure you take notice. Sometimes they feel unhappy with themselves and because you just happen to be around you get the blame. Their anger is really nothing at all to do with you; it is just that you are there.

Sometimes, if your teenagers are siding with someone other than you, it can feel as if they are deliberately trying to hurt you. Sometimes teenagers are able to recognize that giving in to their emotions causes more problems. They find ways to show they are upset and talk to you about their problems without making you feel as if you are the problem.

Living with a teenager can be like living in a soap opera

Many teenagers love watching soap operas. They get addicted to the daily diet of trauma. They identify with favourite characters. They follow the ups and downs of the cast. Soap operas are an escape. They are easy to watch because the plots are simple, the characters are familiar and the language is easy to follow. For many teenagers talking about soap operas is a big part of what they do with their mates. It feels good to have something to share and people to gossip about.

The upside of watching soaps for teenagers is that feeling of belonging and the chance to see life experiences explored. Teenagers can watch the agonies of parenting, the drama and the tedium of relationships, the fun of becoming independent and how people of their age get in and out of difficulties.

The downside of teenagers watching soap operas is that teenagers begin to think that everything has to result in a showdown. Soap operas are full of showdowns. Showdowns are exciting. A showdown involves raised voices, wild threats and stomping off only to come out fighting later on.

Teenagers copy ways of coping with situations that they see portrayed in soap operas. Because they see most events on the screen culminating in a showdown, that is what they expect in real life. Teenagers who watch soaps are being subtly trained to find conflict in almost every situation. They are receiving social training from these programmes. Soap operas are written to attract an audience. Audiences like to watch extreme emotions. Their attention is held when some sort of showdown is in the offing, happening or being gossiped about after the event. It is easy for teenagers to come to believe that all conflict gets dealt with in an argument.

Many teenagers who become trapped by the soap opera mentality are constantly swept along by their heightened emotions.

Katy's world comes to an end – again!

When Katy arrived home late because the bus was held up by road works she was incandescent with fury. Because of this one upset she felt as if her whole life was in ruins. Because of the road works she wouldn't be able to get through the piles of homework she had been given at school, and if she didn't do it her history teacher, whom Katy felt hated her anyway, would have another reason for making Katy's life a misery. Katy said that all her other friends would be able to do the homework because they got a different bus to her. In fact they had probably finished their homework already.

Katy's whole evening could have been spent in emotional turmoil, but when the problem was explored Katy reluctantly realized the reality. The road works had caused her to get home just half an hour later than usual. This amount of time was easy to find in the rest of the evening.

By recognizing the incident for what it was, an irritation, Katy was able to get over her anger. She might have to give herself some time to get back on to an even keel by listening to some music, having a cup of tea or taking the dog out for a walk. She didn't have to let an irritation ruin her night or stop her doing her homework.

How to help teenagers come off the emotional boil

Often the hardest thing to do is to keep a sense of balance when your teenager is in full emotional throttle. The worst thing that you can do is join them in the emotional frenzy.

If the teenager can't control their reaction and wants your attention make sure you are as calm as you can be.

- Sip water rather than strong black coffee.
- Suggest that you both sit down or go for a walk. Doing something together will cut out some of the agitation that gets bounced backwards and forwards when someone prowls around the house or flounces in and out of rooms.
- Try to keep your voice even but don't speak so quietly that you can't be heard.

The stiller you become, the greater the likelihood that you will be able to calm the situation down. You will become calmer if:

- both your feet are flat on the floor;
- you are breathing regularly. Remind yourself of the power of deep breathing;
- you check your fists aren't clenched;
- you flex your fingers;

- you loosen your shoulders;
- you wiggle your toes.

You can also open a window to let some fresh air into the room. Turn off the television or any music so there isn't any noise that stops you from hearing each other.

How to help teenagers come to the point

It can be very helpful to have pencil and paper with you. If you are writing down the problem as you hear it, in point form, it will help you both to clarify just what the issue is.

Seek clarity
When people are upset they often cloud their argument by bringing in all sorts of points that might have nothing to do with the real reason for why they are upset. If you have a pencil and paper and you are writing down the points as your teenager is speaking, both of you have a chance of unpicking the problem. Make sure you can both see what is being written otherwise writing things down can inflame the situation.

Writing things down helps your teenager know that you have a level of detachment. You are listening but not necessarily reacting emotionally to what they are telling you.

Teenagers need to see the power and the usefulness of writing things down. They learn:

- how to follow a strand of an argument. Following an argument is a very useful skill for adult life.
- that what causes emotional turmoil can actually be quite small and easily sorted out.
- that some things are irritating and remain irritating until you get them off your chest, and all that takes is to tell someone.
- those ideas that seem quite simple can be complex.
- how to present information so other people can see your point of view.
- how to simmer down in order that life can carry on.

It's not fair

When some teenagers speak to their parents it is only ever about their grievances. Their constant refrain is, 'It's not fair.'

Olivia made her parents' lives a misery. There was always something Olivia felt should be bought for her or somewhere she should be taken. She would not see how unfair she was being. She was impossible to live with. She would cry, sulk and slam doors in order to force her parents into doing whatever she wanted. When her parents went to bed they would talk about what they could do to try and make Olivia happier and be able to get through this stage.

Part of the problem was that all the teenagers Olivia was mixing with were similar. They spent their lives working out how to get their parents to buy them things. They got no satisfaction from what they were bought because the next time they saw something else they felt they must have, the pressure started all over again. They were fashion victims. Trying to set an allowance hadn't worked because Olivia kept on nagging about what it was reasonable for her to use her allowance for and what she felt her parents should just get her. There were constant discussions about the allowance and it kept being adjusted and new lists of what it was to cover drawn up, but Olivia was never satisfied.

The bottom line

To get out of this endless cycle of the teenager whingeing, you worrying and then you giving in, you have to let your teenager know your bottom line.

A bottom line means everyone knows what is non-negotiable. Without a bottom line, to an immature teenager, everything seems to be up for grabs.

For a teenager who always wants new things and money for activities, you must set a budget. This puts you back in the adult position. You decide how much money your teenager should have and over what period. From then on the decisions are theirs. If you feel confident in yourself and you have set limits, you are giving yourself a protection when the nagging begins. More importantly you are teaching your teenager that progress comes from setting limits and from understanding the limits.

Setting limits

Teenagers need to learn that there is more real choice when there seems to be less choice. If they demand to be given everything they fancy on a whim and that demand is satisfied they are not building the skills that will help them weigh up choices.

Your teenagers may try and make you feel guilty, embarrassed, mean or old fashioned for setting limits but you need to remember that what you are doing is teaching them about real life. Everyone has a right to set their own limits and you want your teenagers to know they have the right to set their own. Adulthood is easier if you have the confidence to set your limits, can recognize the limits that others have set and know how to compromise or look for alternatives.

It's my money

Winston wanted money to go to the pictures. Winston was used to going to his mother, giving her a hug and asking for money. It had always worked. His mother had felt uneasy about this for some time because it didn't feel as though Winston was getting any sense of the value of money. He didn't seem to realize that there was a difference whether he was asking for £2 for a magazine, £5 to go bowling or £20 to go shopping with his mates. This way of operating had crept up on his mum almost without her noticing. They had got into a habit that she felt was not helpful to Winston. She knew that £20 took a lot of earning. Winston didn't seem to understand.

Winston needed to know several things:

- If he was planning on doing something that needed money he had to use his own – lots of teenagers have money from presents but don't think they should spend it.
- If he needed more money he would have to find a way of earning it.

- If he didn't have money he would have to find things to do that didn't cost anything.
- It was his mother's choice which things she paid for and which things she didn't.

Winston would learn how to discriminate. He would learn how to make decisions because he would have a better understanding of what to base his decisions on. He would start to compare. He might compare price against pleasure, time against money, and quality against quantity.

Learning to discriminate for most of us takes a lifetime. Being given chances to practise choice and think about the reasons you made the choices you made is invaluable. As a teenager this extends from deciding what sort of shoes to buy to what sort of friends you will pick. As an adult we may have to exercise choice over what type of treatment to go for when we are ill, what sort of mortgage to get and how much credit we feel we can carry.

Choosing how to make the most out of your life

Learning to make choices means that you can become self-reliant in all areas of your life. You will know what foods will make you fit for work, how much sleep you need if you are going to feel alert, which things you need to restore your energies and which friends to see at different times depending on what resources you have available.

That is that – dealing with nagging

If you remember that you are the adult and it is your right and responsibility to set limits that work for you and that you think will work for your teenager you will be able to cope with your nagging teenager.

- You won't be sucked in and you will be detached.
- When you feel detached you will be able to see the situation clearly.

- When you can see the situation clearly, you won't feel upset when your teenager tries to persuade you to do something that you know you have decided against.
- You will be able to take a deep breath and know that this is an important learning stage. You have set the limit.
- If your teenager says they want more you have simply and calmly to remind them that you have given them what you have decided they can have.

It is important not to negotiate until the nagging has stopped. If you try to negotiate with a teenager who thinks there is something to be gained from nagging you will find yourself back where you started.

Remember:

- Keep your adult position.
- It is reasonable to set limits.
- The limit you have set is reasonable.

He drives me mad

Robert was always in trouble. He was his own worst enemy although he thought any adult who was expecting him to behave reasonably was the actual enemy. He was always pulling faces. The faces were to show that whatever he was being asked to do was stupid. He would pull a face if he were asked to set the table, dragging himself around as though he was the 'missing link'.

The effect on anyone who was trying to do anything with him was dramatic. No matter how hard they tried to stay calm they couldn't help getting irritated by Robert's antics. Within seconds they would find themselves banging things down and moaning at Robert. This would make no difference and in the end they would tell him to go away.

At school Robert constantly fiddled, drew on his hands, doodled all over his work and flicked things. His messing about was off-putting for teachers and anyone trying to work with him. His hands and nails were often filthy. He would pick scabs on his arms and legs. The blood from his scabs would end up all over the place, on his shirt, on his books and over his hands. He turned what should have been quite straightforward into a series of hurdles. No matter how often it was explained to Robert that he was driving people mad he couldn't stop his silly behaviour.

Robert would complain that the work at school was stupid and his teachers were stupid as well. He moaned about what he had to do but he couldn't get himself into a state where he could get help. At home he didn't finish his homework because the time to do it just ran out. Sometimes, if the work did get done, he forgot to take it into school. If he got it into school he forgot to hand it in. He left a trail of debris wherever he had been.

What is your problem?

When a teenager is behaving in a way where all the reactions they get from other people are negative, they need help to work out where the problem is coming from.

Too tired to think
Sometimes teenagers get into this hopeless state because they are too tired. Some teenagers don't realize that rest is as important a part of being able to function as eating the right food. They think staying up late is adult. They think life after ten o'clock at night has a mystery and romance about it.

Affected by food
Sometimes teenagers get into this state because of what they have eaten. For some individuals some foods can have a strange effect. The food can make them dozy or cross. What they have eaten may affect how quickly their brain can work.

Some foods may make some people feel uncomfortable. They find it hard to get to sleep because of what they have eaten and any sleep that they do get is not very restful. Some foods make some people feel agitated. They become jumpy and unsettled.

Wound up

Sometimes teenagers get into this state because they let other people wind them up. They may not even realize that it is someone else egging them on to behave in such a ludicrous way. They think they are being part of a crowd. They haven't realized that others will pull back to avoid getting into trouble.

This often happens to teenagers who are the youngest in the class. At Parents' Evenings teachers may observe that the young person seems to like being the class clown or getting everyone to laugh. What is really going on is that because the individual getting into trouble is so much younger than many of the others in the class he wants to be accepted and he thinks his only way of doing that is to get people to laugh.

Some teenagers are too vulnerable when they move school. They are like eager puppies wanting everyone to know that they want to be their friends. They will mess about hoping to attract some people to like them.

Feeling worthless

Sometimes teenagers get into this state because they feel worthless. It can happen when there is a breakdown in the family, if a teenager is being bullied or if they are being abused.

Let's sort it out

What all teenagers need to know is that help can only be given if they are in a state to receive help. To be in a state to receive help they have to recognize that there is a problem.

Sleep

If someone is over-tired they need to work out a way of getting more sleep. People's sleep patterns differ. Even within families the amount of sleep and when people sleep can vary hugely. You can help your teenager find a balance that suits them. For one teenager getting up at six to do homework might just suit whereas another may prefer to stay up late to get the homework done and catch up on sleep at the weekends. Other people can put their head down for five or ten minutes and wake up with enough energy to keep going.

Food

If someone is eating something that affects their behaviour you can usually tell because they have bad days and good days that can't be accounted for by anything else. On a bad day they might be:

- very bad tempered
- lethargic
- aggressive
- depressed
- clumsy
- disorganized
- argumentative.

More and more people are noticing that food can affect their mood. If you think that your teenager's moods might be being affected by the foods that they are eating it is a good idea to keep a record. Whenever there is an inexplicable change in their mood make a list of the foods that they have eaten in the last eight hours. Keep the list and the next time there is another change in behaviour make a new list. You will start to see that the moods can be associated with particular foods. For some people it is only one or two foods that cause them a problem and these will be easy for them to cut out of their diet.

The important thing for your teenager to know is that they can control their mood swings if they can control their food. It can be very worrying for a teenager to think that they have personality problems when the problems are simply coming from what they have eaten. It is worth checking.

Clowning around

The best way to help a teenager who is young and finding it hard to cope socially is to ask him or her how they want to be seen by their friends and teachers. The list can include positive and negative qualities:

sensible	hard working	rude
resourceful	outgoing	silly

| comical | daring | polite |
| ridiculous | irritating | mature. |

When your teenager decides how they want to be seen then you can talk through their choices. If all their choices are negative you can explore why they have decided they should only be seen as difficult. If there is a mixture of positive and negative qualities then you can talk about why a negative quality might cause people to overlook their positive qualities. If they choose only positive qualities then you can ask them how someone would know they were the sort of person they want to appear.

Self-esteem

Sometimes teenagers can feel bullied by a situation and no one else realizes that the teenager is suffering. Many teenagers find coping with the demands of being a teenager at the same time as trying to cope with big changes in their lives, exhausting and overwhelming. Their bodies are changing. The demands at school are changing. Their friends might be changing and maybe their parents' partners are changing as well. They feel as though all the adjustments have to be made by them. No one is helping them to cope.

Teenagers do still need input from their parents, because they are still learning. They may need information about how to do something that must be done. More often they need strategies that they can then use to become self-sufficient and self-reliant. Sometimes they need insights from others to help them get over barriers that come from their own behaviour or from the way they see things.

Teenagers need help to learn how to deal with their life as calmly as possible. They need ways to cope with conflict, whether the conflict is outside them or whether they have conflicting feelings inside.

The outcome of living your life in conflict is a desperate need for reassurance or a desperate need to escape.

The outcome of living your life calmly is a realistic acceptance of changes, challenges and choices.

Work out what is worth worrying about

What teenagers need to learn is that every situation can't be sorted out in the same way. It is important for teenagers to recognize:

- the difference between the things it is worth spending time thinking about because you might be able to sort them out and the things that might go wrong and be irritating, but are just part of life and not worth spending time worrying about.
- that finding fault with the performance or behaviour of someone else does not alter the responsibility they have for getting on with what needs to be done.
- that life is much easier if they approach it with optimism rather than pessimism.
- when they find something hard or uncomfortable they don't have to give up.
- it is okay to be upset about what has happened but that doesn't have to stop them from doing anything else.

Do you really need to moan?

Teenagers who don't learn how to deal with the things that happen in their lives become a pain to other people and to themselves. They can't tell the difference between things that people will want to help them with and things that hardly deserve a mention.

Most of us know people who can't tell the difference between the serious and the trivial. Every incident in their lives can be used, if they feel like it, as a reason for feeling unhappy or aggrieved or outraged. Life, for them, is one long series of disappointments. Even if you really enjoy their company you begin to avoid them because you can never be sure that an evening meant for relaxation and companionship won't be turned into a grand battle between your friend and whomever your friend feels upset with.

You don't have to put up with it

Jane stopped accepting offers to go out for a meal with her old school friend after sitting through yet another uncomfortable

71

evening. If her friend wasn't complaining about the service in the restaurant and asking to speak to the manager she was regaling Jane with all her tales of other battles she had had that week with shop assistants, the staff at work, the people at the gym, the mobile phone company and the council. Jane did not want the feeling that she was supporting her friend in these attacks or that she was being forced to distance herself when what she wanted was an evening where she felt in harmony with her old friend. It was easier to give up going out with her friend than to cope with the irritation she felt as the evening slid into one long moan.

Teenagers notice

Teenagers want the approval of their parents. They will try and be the person they think their parents want. They watch what their parents do more than they listen to what they say. It is worth checking whether what you are doing is unintentionally being an unhelpful model for your teenager.

If your teenager is full of doom and gloom . . .
Check how you speak when something goes wrong. Teenagers can pick up unhelpful habits from their parents. This does not matter that much if they pick up plenty of helpful ones as well, but sometimes they can seem to home in on our less effective ways of carrying on without us even realizing that they have picked up an unhelpful habit from us.

When Sara's mum overheard Sara moaning endlessly about the state of the buses she realized where some of Sara's negative views about the world had come from.

If your teenager makes sweeping derogatory statements about things you know they don't really know about . . .
Check how often you simply agree with negative statements your teenagers make when you have no way of knowing whether what they have said is true or not.

Jack's dad found himself agreeing about how awful Jack's physics teacher was at explaining about electricity. He even told other people how hopeless Jack's teachers all were. He pulled himself up short when one day, about to tell yet another person how awful the school was, he realized that he had not even met Jack's teacher let alone sat in a class while he explained electricity, so really he had no way of knowing whether the chap was any good or not. He had no evidence about the school at all. He had simply been listening to his fifteen-year-old and gone along with that.

If your teenager puts lots of things in the 'too hard basket' and won't try again even with help . . .
Check whether you give up when things go wrong.

6

Surviving inner turmoil

Life is a mixture of the happy, the sad, the extraordinary, the ordinary, the routine and the unexpected.

It is a mixture of good health, poor health, birth and death.

It is a mixture of the complicated, the straightforward, the difficult and the easy.

It is a mixture of the hurtful and the downright terrifying.

Some things can be planned for and other things can just happen. Some things can be organized while other things can't be.

It's too hard

Mostly we can cope with what happens but every so often there is a trauma.

A trauma is when everything that you have learned isn't enough to help you cope with the situation in front of you. It is an event that you can feel you will never learn enough to be able to cope with. What makes something a trauma for one person does not make a trauma for someone else. In this chapter you will find suggestions for ways you can cope when strong feelings overwhelm you.

A strong emotional reaction can be frightening because you can feel completely taken over by it. You can feel as if normal life is a thing of the past and you will never be like other people again.

You are not alone

- Although you feel isolated other people will be having just as intense reactions to things that have happened to them.
- Although it will take time you will gradually be able to cope as you see again that life is a mixture.
- The strongest emotions come when what we thought was reasonable or what we have fought long and hard for is brought to a sudden end. The more unlikely the thing that happens, the more severe is the reaction.
- The sudden death of a young person is far less likely than the death at an old age of someone else. Our reaction to the first is often more extreme because of the unexpectedness of it.
- Coping with the feelings you have when your child is very ill can be overwhelming. Parents want and expect their children to be healthy. The unexpectedness of the situation when a child falls ill, affects your reactions.

Emotional upheaval

People feel overwhelmed by emotions for different reasons. It is natural to feel ripped apart by some things. It is obvious that this extreme reaction will change to something else with time. We hear people talk about things that have happened to them which were horrifying and horrible. We know that they have found some way of living even when they have suffered things that we feel we could never deal with.

Things that go wrong and how they make us feel
- Loss and change can cause you to feel grief-stricken, frightened, unstable, lonely, unable to cope.
- Betrayal and deceit can cause you to feel isolated, worthless, foolish and used.
- Having the right to be who you are threatened or destroyed can leave you feeling powerless and hopeless.
- Disappointment can make you feel anxious, confused and angry.

- Rejection can make you feel inadequate, worthless, hopeless and terrified.
- Meanness from anybody can make you feel disconcerted, exploited, gullible and manipulated.
- Failure can make you feel like a fraud and ridiculous, as though you have betrayed the trust of others.
- If anyone close to you whom you feel you know and understand causes intentional pain to someone else you can feel grief, guilt, despair and shock.
- How you react will be unique and you are entitled to your reactions.

When terrible things make us feel distressed

Your mind can be very clear when something terrible happens. You know what has happened and you can tell other people what has happened. They can ask you questions about it and you can think of answers. At the time when something goes wrong people realize that you are in need. They can be pretty sure that what they are offering, you will find helpful.

As time goes on the impact of the event on your life is changing all the time. Some days the impact is high, others it is not as high. You gradually feel you can do some things and you want to do others. This is a harder time because it is not clear to the people who care about you what sort of support you need. It is not clear to you either what sort of support you want. It is unpredictable. You can't tell from one day to the next how you are going to be feeling or what it is that you will want.

Because a trauma can throw you so completely, as you start to pick up the pieces you may not realize how haphazard you are being. You might be doing some things really well and some things not at all. You might be doing most things but not in the way you used to. That makes it hard for those supporting you. They don't know where you need help. They could come in and offer help and you could feel they were interfering, or you could feel very grateful. You could need help but feel too exhausted to take the help. You could feel upset if it is offered and upset if it is not.

People who are trying to help you can be confused if you still need help but you seem to be getting on with your life at the same time. They might feel that you are taking advantage of them, but really you need all the help you can get. You might feel that they are slowing your recovery down by always treating you as though you can't do anything for yourself or always expecting that you will be sad. The problem is that it is unexplored territory for everyone.

For everyone it is a hazardous trip. Everyone feels vulnerable. No one wants to put a foot wrong. People will get it wrong because things are changing so subtly all the time. As long as there is goodwill, mistakes can be sorted out some time.

What is goodwill?

Goodwill is a generosity of spirit that allows individuals to be who they are without rejecting them.

To allow people to be who they are, even if what they are doing seems difficult to understand or agree with, you can:

- put things 'on hold'. Give them time and space to work something out. Accept they are having a bad time that will pass when they can cope.
- find something to do that will demonstrate that you care without intruding.
- accept that they might doubt you because they doubt everything at the time.
- accept that they will find their own way through which might mean that they change their life completely.
- keep reminding yourself of what is in your own life – your window box, the course you are doing, the walks you take and the memories that you have.

When you develop generosity of spirit it leads to developing wisdom.

What is wisdom?

Wisdom is using the capacity

- to see the fundamentals that all human beings share;
- to appreciate differences;
- to recognize that things are complex and not expect simple solutions;
- to see the simple in the complex;
- to see that even in the midst of horror there is beauty and that even when things are looking hopeless you may spot the chance for a change.

How to be wise: the A–Z of wisdom

Attention. When you pay attention to the matter in hand, no matter how small that is, you are putting your mind into the best position there is. You are giving your mind the opportunity to work effectively.

Believing. If you believe that you can do it you will do it.

Choices. A wise person makes choices because of what they know rather than because of the persuasive techniques of someone else.

Discipline. Limiting your attention to what is needed means that you don't waste any of your resources.

Enquiry. A wise person seeks the best answer in any situation and knows that an answer in one situation is not necessarily the answer in every situation.

Forgiveness. Without forgiveness your life is limited. A wise person knows that you can only move on if you forgive yourself.

Grace. By being gracious a wise person is able to see the best that can be done.

Harmony. A wise person creates harmony by being still, not judging and by recognizing that others have depth.

Intelligence. Intelligence comes when you can tell the difference between what is needed and what isn't.

Joy. A wise person can see things that are available as delightful.

Keen. You strip away all the clutter and see the quality that lies inside.

Love. If you love someone you tolerate his or her right to be. You might not tolerate what they are doing but you do tolerate their right to be living their life.

Meditation. A wise person knows that they need to be able to go still and empty their mind. There are many ways of finding that stillness but the stillness needs to be found.

Nature. A wise person lives the cycles that are part of the human condition.

Open. An open person who is wise welcomes ideas, thoughts and events and measures them against what they know is the truth.

Patience. A wise person knows that over time there is a balance.

Quality. A wise person knows that everything has its own quality. Fine qualities are the ones they seek and want to hold.

Reality. A wise person accepts that all people will be making choices. They have the right to make choices and those choices have to be allowed.

Selflessness. A wise person will look at what needs to be done and how best to do it without thinking how it will reflect on them.

Truthfulness. A wise person knows that the truth will stand the test of time.

Unity. A wise person knows that whatever the superficial differences appear to be there will be a way of finding a common understanding.

Vitality. A wise person knows that running through everything there is a life force. It is the life force that keeps us going on even when we feel like giving up. The life force keeps going no matter what is happening.

Work. A wise person knows that work is essential. The most important work you do is to search for wisdom.

eXamples. The wise person knows that how he or she behaves influences the way other people behave.

Youthfulness. A wise person stays in touch with the joy and excitement of youth.

Zetetic. A wise person will be a zetetic. You will continually search after truth.

How to do something about your feelings

If you feel worthless:

- Choose something to do for yourself. The act of choosing will mean you are giving yourself some value. It could be buying yourself a present or deciding to read a book. It could be having a bath, watching a video or playing a computer game.

If you feel grief-stricken:

- Buy a plant as a focus for fond memories of what has gone.
- Compile a photo album of your memories. It doesn't matter if you sob and wail while you do this. You will feel comforted and

less bereft as you realize that memories are for ever.
- Write an A–Z of words that you associate with what you want to remember. The words could be places, people, feelings, possessions, foods, events – anything that you shared.

If you feel frightened:

- Write down the things that you can do. When you have written ten you will realize that you can still handle lots of things in your life.

If you feel unstable:

- Read some poetry.
- Pray.

If you feel lonely:

- Find a café where you can sit and read a book or a paper or just watch the comings and goings. Be interested in conversations you overhear. Think about the lives of the people you see. What did they eat for breakfast? Which person in the café do you think got to work late this morning?

If you feel unable to cope:

- Put on your favourite cheerful music and hum, dance or sing along.
- Do something repetitive. Polish, clean, dig, weed or walk.

If you feel isolated:

- Make a point of saying hello to someone. Don't worry if your voice sounds strange to you. It is important to make a contact otherwise you can feel as if you will never risk speaking to anyone again.
- Choose a friendly bank, go to a small post office. Find ways of interacting on a level that you like.

If you feel foolish:

- Remember that the person who never made a mistake never made anything.
- Look at the things that have gone right, where you have made good judgments. Do you have any favourite clothes? Well the decision to buy those was a good one. Do you have a comfortable pair of shoes? Well, picking those was a good thing. Have you ever cooked something and eaten far more of it than you meant to because it tasted so good. Well, that means you know how to cook. Has anyone ever asked you for advice or information on something they want to do? Well, they asked you because they felt you were competent enough to help them.

If you feel used:

- Make a genuine gift where you will never know how it has been received. Buy a tin of cat food and put it in the RSPCA collection bin at the shops. Take some books to the book bank. Clear a cupboard and take what you don't need to the charity shop. You are a generous person so don't let one bad experience take that pleasure away.

If you feel powerless:

- Try moving at a different pace. If you tend to walk quickly, deliberately slow yourself down. If you usually move slowly, then speed up. The feeling that you can change what you do, even in the simplest way, will help you to regain a sense of self control.

If you feel hopeless:

- Do something simple like a jigsaw puzzle or a crossword or even some colouring in. Something that you know you can do. Don't dismiss it as too easy to be significant. Enjoy it for enjoyment's sake.

If you feel anxious:

- Slow your breathing down. Light a candle and then steadily blow at the flame but not so hard you will blow the flame out. Keep blowing until you need to breathe in. This will calm your breathing and your body. Don't worry if the candle blows out, you can always light it again.

If you feel confused:

- Go to the library and find a book that has a title that appeals. As you start to read, your attention will be taken to your quite straightforward reactions to what you are reading. Let yourself follow the structure that the author has provided.
- Follow the instructions to make something like a cake. Not a complicated recipe but something where you are acting under simple instruction.

If you feel angry:

- You could use up the energy. Go for a fast walk or swim fifty lengths. You could punch a pillow.
- Read some jokes or watch a funny video. Have some funny tapes to play.

If you feel inadequate:

- You might be expecting too much of yourself. Don't try to be perfect and don't expect that what needs to be done has to be done perfectly.
- Write down ten things you have to do. If you can't think of ten see that as a plus. Then put the ten things into order of importance. They must come one after the other. You can't decide that they are all as important as each other. One has to come first, at the top of the list, and one has to be last. You will be helping yourself realize that everything doesn't have to be perfect and everything doesn't have to be done at once.

If you feel terrified:

- Make a list of all the things that might happen. You will start off by putting down all the dreadful things you imagine. Now think of as many positive or ordinary things as you have negatives. At first you might not be able to think of any but gradually you will. You will be training yourself to be more balanced when you think about the future. Yes, there are many terrifying things that could happen but they are balanced by wonderful and ordinary things that happen too.

If you feel disconcerted:

- You need to take a step back and look at the situation again. You will be disconcerted because something you expected hasn't happened in the way you expected. Think about what you were expecting. Although you can feel very surprised and confused, once you think about what it was that was not the way you expected, you will normally find it is quite a small detail. Once you recognize the detail you will begin to feel less disconcerted and more settled.

If you feel exploited:

- You will be kicking yourself for having let the situation turn out the way it has. You may well have stuck to something in the face of all the evidence. It could be that the other person has spotted a weakness in you and has behaved without integrity. It could be that you have ignored the evidence and banked on something that you had no proof actually existed. In order to stop beating yourself up and berating yourself for having got into a position where you could be exploited see it as a learning experience.

If you feel gullible:

- Instead of thinking of how easily you can be taken in think of the advice you would give somebody else in the same situation.

You could write it as a letter and then you can get it out and remind yourself of how clearly you can think. You can write more than one letter as your thoughts become clearer.

If you feel manipulated:

• Take some time to go somewhere and sit quietly. Feel for at least a few moments that you are not being at someone else's beck and call.

If you feel fraudulent:

• You may feel as if you have let someone down. In the future work out what time you really have to offer to do things. Try doubling the time you need to get somewhere and halving the time you can give someone. That way you give yourself a bit of leeway to meet your commitments and cope with anything that might crop up that you haven't planned for. Demands on our time are constantly changing and if we agree to use all our time over an extended period we are likely to make mistakes, become ill, feel depressed or feel inadequate.

If you feel ridiculous:

• Take the empty bottles to the bottle bank.
• Take the old newspapers to the recycling bin.
• Throw out or give away something you know makes you look silly.

If you feel treacherous:

• If you have betrayed a confidence or gossiped about somebody you care about you may feel you need to tell the person what you have done.
• Decide that in future, if you are someone who gets stuck for something to say, you will notice what other people say to you that leaves them able to be the nice people they are, and then

pick up tips. If the conversation does veer dangerously close to you saying something you will regret almost immediately, make an excuse and go to the loo or nip out to buy a paper or go and put the kettle on. When you get back the conversation will have moved on or you will have a fresh perspective.

• Try to remember that you don't have to get people to like you by agreeing or even adding something to the conversation.

If you feel invisible:

• Book a haircut or have a massage. Do something where someone tends to you. Take time out to notice that you really do exist.

If you haven't got much time, quick ways to feel fresh and more able to cope are:

• splashing or spraying your face with water;
• spraying on some perfume or after-shave;
• washing your hands;
• having a shower;
• having a drink of water;
• emptying a bin;
• eating a piece of fruit;
• washing up a cup;
• ironing a tee shirt.

These suggestions are not meant to be flippant but just to remind you that taking control of something, no matter how small, will help you move from seeing everything as going wrong to seeing something going right.

People for generations have used putting the kettle on and making a cup of tea as a way of creating a space and a diversion that doesn't minimize the seriousness of the emotions but does give a prop, even if you are doing it just for yourself.

7

When teenagers say 'No!'

It is important that parents and teenagers realize that without meaning to they can undermine each other's sense of self-worth. The way they ask each other questions or make requests and the way they respond to questions or requests will have a profound effect on how they feel, and how the person they are speaking to feels as well. Parents of teenagers have spent more than ten years making big and small decisions for their children. Teenagers now need to start making decisions for themselves.

There will be tension. There may be arguments.

This chapter will give you ways to tackle those points of tension and ways to ask for what you want.

Did you hear what I said?

When someone doesn't do what you have asked, you can feel:

- angry
- powerless
- fed up
- silly
- overwhelmed
- a failure
- irritated
- calm
- interested
- hurt
- critical
- fearful.

When Jody and her husband invited the new neighbours in for coffee their daughter Rosie was eager to meet them too. Rosie was hoping that she could make friends with their son who seemed to be roughly the same age. The son didn't come round with them but Rosie still joined in the chat about the area, schools and so on. She enjoyed the conversation and thought their new neighbours seemed interesting people. Her mum suddenly remembered some photographs she had taken of the area a few years earlier and asked Rosie if she could pop upstairs to fetch the box they were in. Then they could show them to the new neighbours whom she was sure would be interested. Rosie refused. She began by ignoring the request but when her mum asked again she said she wouldn't go and fetch them and they were boring anyway.

Rosie's mum felt confusion at first, followed quickly by anger. She felt let down by Rosie and embarrassed. What she felt was a reasonable request had suddenly become a Molotov cocktail. The daughter she had felt was her friend had become her adversary. She felt shocked and betrayed.

Rosie herself could hardly believe the words that were coming out of her mouth and was devastated when she saw the look on her mother's face, but she wasn't going to give in.

I'm not a servant

This is a situation many parents meet as their teenagers see growing up as becoming equal. Equality to teenagers means not having to be singled out to be the servant of other people or be discounted, compared to other people present. Teenagers are happy to help one moment and the next moment are sickened when they think they are being expected to be a servant when they thought they were being a friend. Teenagers should be getting a sense of their own value and can be sensitive to anything that challenges the value they are putting on themselves.

There can be many reasons why teenagers don't do what you have asked.

- They haven't heard you.
- They don't understand you.
- They don't see the point of what you have asked.
- They don't agree with you.
- They don't think they can do what you have asked.
- They don't see why they should.
- They don't see why you should be the person asking them.
- They want to embarrass you.
- They want to show off.

Why do you want them to do what you have asked?

- To be a part of what is going on.
- Because you need their help.
- The job needs more than one pair of hands.
- They are better at it than you.
- They have the time and you don't.
- To be ready on time.
- To get something finished.
- To enable you to get on with something else.

Why do you think they should do what you have asked?

- They should respect your wishes.
- They should behave reasonably.
- It's only fair to share the tasks.
- You've done what they wanted.
- You've been good to them.
- To prevent an argument.

If they refuse to do what you have asked you can respond in the following ways:

- Tell them how you feel.
- Tell them how that makes them look.
- Ask them how they feel.

Becoming independent means realizing you can say 'No' as well as 'Yes'

As children become teenagers they realize that there are differences in the relationship with their parents. At one moment they may want their approval and so they will agree to everything they are asked. At another time they may want their independence and start to say 'No'. It depends on how they see the situation. This can confuse parents because they feel that the teenager should know that if they meet with their parents' approval the pay-off is their independence.

Independent

Craig wanted to be allowed to go to see his local football team when they played away. Although his parents were worried about the trip they felt that Craig had handled going to see his team play home games so well that they could trust him to be more independent. Craig's parents were confident that Craig knew how to keep out of trouble and whoever they asked to take him along with their group wouldn't have a problem with him.

Still a child

Mark, on the other hand, went to the match but didn't come home at the time he said he would and when he did come in was full of tales of having to flee from the opposing fans, seeing police sorting out fights, and things that he had shouted at other people at the match. Mark's parents didn't feel they could give permission for him to join the fans when they went to see an away match. They felt that he wasn't in control of himself and it wouldn't be fair to ask anyone else to be in control of him.

Craig could look after himself while Mark was still behaving like a child.

Looking after yourself

If children have learnt how to look out for themselves when they are young, they should know how to look out for themselves when they have more independence. Children who are happy to get into scrapes, lose their keys and forget where they are going because they know someone else will sort it out will get into just as many scrapes when they are older, but there won't be as many people there to sort it out.

It's your choice

When children are little they do demonstrate their independence and their individuality but we are less likely to be hurt by it than we are when they are older. A child choosing to spend all their pocket money on sweets or their whole holiday money on a ridiculous cuddly toy doesn't cut us to the quick. We may be interested in the choices they make and fascinated by what takes their interest and what they see as important, but we do not feel discounted or unloved if they choose a toy that is not the one we suggest, or pick some sweets that we think aren't good value for money. We tend to see these moments of independence as the child learning and that if they have made a choice that we don't think is right they will come to see it more sensibly in the future.

When teenagers show their independence and their individuality by refusing to do what has been asked, we can feel very upset. This is because we have built up an image in our minds of the relationship we have with them. This image will include things like respect, friendship and understanding. By doing what we have asked they bolster up that image. They reassure us that what we think about the strength of the relationship is true. If they refuse to do what we want we feel as if the relationship or our image of the relationship is in jeopardy or has been blown apart.

I'm just not going to do it

It had always been Ashley's job to empty the dishwasher. Other members of the family had other jobs and this was the job Ashley did. He had been thrilled when it was decided he was old enough to do it on his own. Over the years the novelty had worn off for him but he still did the job without any fuss or complaining. He just did it.

The family operated very much as a team and it felt to his mum and dad that they had obviously organized the jobs well and brought their children up to be responsible for their bit of family life. It was therefore quite a shock when Ashley said he wasn't going to empty the dishwasher anymore. He couldn't see the point of putting things away only for them to be taken out again. He didn't want to spend his life doing a task that was futile and unnecessary.

His dad thought he would just have a chat with him and explain why everybody had to help. He thought maybe there was another job Ashley could do and things could settle down again.

The discussion with Ashley didn't go as planned. Ashley did not feel there was another job he could do because he felt that all housework was a waste of time, especially as there were more important things to be getting steamed up about. He couldn't believe the only thing his parents were interested in was whether the dishwasher had been emptied or not. Didn't they care about the wars happening around the globe or the parts of the rainforest that were being bulldozed for profit? His father retreated wondering whether he would have the time to empty the dishwasher himself.

As the days went on and Ashley stuck to his guns his parents felt upset and disappointed. They either emptied the dishwasher them-selves or asked one of the other children to do it, but to them it felt as if the family life they had created was starting to break down. Suddenly they realized that the life they had created was open to question and was being questioned. They couldn't work out how to explain to Ashley that they weren't being selfish or thinking that they were superior to other people but it was more complicated than that when you were an adult. To Ashley it was simple. His parents were small-minded and he wasn't going to be caught in the same trap as them.

Relationships shift, not shatter

It is important to see incidents such as these as the relationship your teenager has with the family shifting rather than shattering. The relationship will continue to shift into adulthood. Inevitably each member of the family will find ways of becoming who they want to be and will learn how to allow others to be the people they are.

When children grow older we can often see the choices they make and the way they choose to demonstrate their independence as risky. When they reject what we suggest or advise we aren't sure just how they want the relationship to be now or in the future. We are not sure just what responsibility we still have. It is a constant adjustment.

Infringement of liberty or an invitation to shine and share

Teenagers often respond to someone asking them to do something as if the request is an infringement of their liberty. They develop stock responses that can be:

- No.
- What can I get out of it?
- Why can't you ask someone else?

As teenagers mature they realize that they can get enjoyment out of the most mundane task and unexpected pleasure from something that they didn't want to do. They realize that how you feel about what you do depends on how open you are to the possibilities of any situation.

If you want anything just ask

In the course of a day adults will be asked to do many things. We will veer in our responses to those requests from quite happy to quite upset. We may occasionally be neutral but more often than not there will be some emotion that we feel at the point of being asked. These emotions may range from delight to despair. Our response to these requests may make us sound enthusiastic or rude. They could make us look helpful and willing or thunderous. They can make us appear energetic or lethargic. The way we have reacted can make others feel supported, comforted, condemned or exhausted. It is worth thinking of all the different ways you feel when you are asked to do something.

Adults have feelings too

Excited

Jenny was delighted to be asked to be on the swimming committee. Up until now she had just been one of the mums whose children were in the team, but now she would get the chance to help with some of the planning. She knew the skills she had would be of benefit. She wouldn't have put herself forward but she was delighted to be asked.

Respected

Peter was asked if he could give a talk to the sixth form at the local school about the marathon he had trained for and completed in the summer. He suddenly recognized that what he had done had earned him respect. He was being asked to give the talk because of what he had done.

Valued

Kiera was asked by a friend to sit with her mother who had Alzheimer's. Her friend never asked anyone for help so Kiera knew she was valued as a friend when she was asked.

Neutral

Each week somebody has to collect the boys from swimming. Whoever is asked just does it. It fits in okay and it has to be done.

Irritated

After working hard all day David arrived home to find a message on the answer machine asking him to get the dinner ready. There were some people coming round later for a meal and Sadie had been held up in traffic. David felt irritated. He had planned on a leisurely shower before the guests arrived. Now there was no chance to wind down at all.

Resentful

Laura hated it when her sister would ask her to look after the children when she went for a city break. Laura knew that she would feel resentful all day as she looked after the kids and imagined her sister swanning round the shops, but she didn't know how to say 'No'.

Proud

When Kevin was promoted at work he was asked to give the vote of thanks to the speaker at the company dinner. He felt proud of himself for working his way up to where he was now, at the level where the company asked him to represent them.

Used

You can feel used when your teenagers ask you to drive them to the pictures but never ask if you would like to see the film too or even say 'Thank you'.

Useful

You can feel useful if someone is doing something and you are included as part of the team to get the thing done. When teenagers are going away you can feel useful when they ask for your help with the packing or your advice on which route to take.

Needed

Oliver was a keen computer buff and was thrilled when his son's school asked him to design a website for the school. They knew that he had sophisticated skills and they needed the best website they could have, so they asked him.

Excluded

Stacey was asked if she would help at the dancing class concert and she said she would. When she arrived she was asked to look after people handing in their coats in the cloakroom. As she went off to get started she saw everyone else busy in the kitchen putting out refreshments and laughing and chatting. She had to get on with her job on her own while the others had the companionship of a group while they worked. She felt left out, awkward and friendless.

Nervous

When Sean was asked to chair a meeting of local residents who were upset about the proposed installation of a mobile phone mast in the area he felt very nervous. Although he was angry about the proposed mast and wanted to do his bit he hated the idea of having to chair a meeting, especially one where tempers might get heated.

Tired

Sometimes the overwhelming feeling we get when we are asked to do something is exhaustion. Maybe we have done the job just too many times in the past. Perhaps we don't feel we can do it and the idea of having to just makes us want to go straight to bed.

Put out

When you are trying to plan your life and feel you have got a balance or found some space for yourself and then you are asked to do something which will mean that what you have planned can't be done, you can feel very put out. The same request at another time may not cause you a problem at all because you feel differently then, but just at the moment you haven't got the space.

Surprised

Being surprised when you are asked to do something means that you are unprepared for the request. You may be able to do it or you may not be able to do it, but you had not thought that you would be asked.

Apprehensive

You think you can do it but you are not sure. You could feel apprehensive when you were asked to present a report. Part of the apprehension comes from not being sure how to cope with the unpredictable.

Even with all the experience that adults have had, in order to cope in a reasonable way with the demands that are made of them, they have to work hard. They think about their feelings. People who can cope often have ways of giving themselves a little breathing space to consider the request.

How to get some breathing space

These strategies work for adults and teenagers. They allow the person being asked to weigh up their priorities.

1. Ask for clarification.

    * How long will it take?
    * What is involved?
    * Who else is doing it?
    * Who could be called on to help?
    * How urgent is it?

2. Tell the person when you will get back to them with an answer. Don't always feel you must give an immediate yes or no.

3. Say that you will have to check with someone else or with your diary/timetable.

4. Ask them to repeat the request. You get the chance to hear it again and maybe notice something you have missed. Often if someone has made a request in quite a blunt or even rude way, just saying pardon to them means that the person says it again but with a bit more balance or adding in a please.

5. Ask them to do something while you are thinking or doing what they asked. 'Could you take the rubbish out or put the kettle on while I am having a look?' This turns it into teamwork rather than stress.

Reasonable and unreasonable requests

It is a fact of life that when teenagers are feeling vulnerable for whatever reason they can see any request made by you, no matter how reasonable, as an unreasonable demand. By the same token they see any request made to you, no matter how unreasonable, as perfectly reasonable.

You can teach your teenagers about asking and responding to requests. If they can learn how to deal with any suggestion or request made to them politely, helpfully and sensibly they will have wonderful life skills for the future.

8

Being alone need not be lonely

It is hard not to panic if your teenager doesn't have friends. Social pressure to be seen as popular affects parents almost as much as it does their teenagers. Teenagers who struggle to make friends can find making friends easier as their social circle widens when they become adult. Teenagers who seem to be anti-social or clumsy in social situations usually grow into adults who manage their lives as happily as most.

Discerning not desperate

Most people like to have friends although some people prefer their own company. The aim always, whatever your age, is to be discerning about the sort of people whom you associate with. You want to find people who fit the life you think matters.

Parents can feel desperate as their children go through their teenage years trying to find people with whom to be friends. Teenagers are more likely to be discerning if they know that being alone, feeling friendless or feeling lonely is a part of life. Some teenagers think that being alone means they are lonely and friendless. They can't settle to do anything by themselves. They are desperate to be with someone so they feel confident that they are okay. Other teenagers are happy to be alone but not sure whether that makes them weird. They don't find pleasure in unending teenage talk or they have other things they want to do.

Many teenagers find that when they leave school they start to make more friends. They feel that now they have the freedom to choose the type of people they like. That possibility didn't seem to be there at school. For other teenagers who may have found friendships at school easy, this post-school period can be quite traumatic. They have to use skills that they didn't need before. In the social situation of school, making friends just seemed to happen.

People need friends for different reasons

People may need friends:

- for company
- for support
- because they want to have someone to look after
- because they want to be looked after
- for protection
- to show the world that they are popular
- to get a glimpse of another life
- to talk to
- to share an interest with
- because they think they should have a friend
- to explore.

Teenagers are experimenting all the time to find a way of dealing with each challenge that comes up in their lives. Learning how to make, break and keep relationships can be a difficult but in the end positive part of the teenage experience.

Children who don't want friends or who find themselves without friends at any particular time don't have to miss out on all of the experiences that teenagers have although sometimes they think they will. Many of the experiences teenagers think everyone else is having are probably more talked about than done.

Sometimes when teenagers join a group they think is exciting or cool they find that the reality is less interesting than they originally thought. Some teenagers don't recognize the friendship they've got.

Nobody loves me . . .

When Rosie was fourteen she felt as though she had no friends at all. She had been difficult since she was seven when her mother had remarried. Rosie thought that she would feel okay if people showed her that they loved her. She felt unloved and friendless and whenever she got upset would always wail about the fact that nobody loved her and nobody cared about her. She would say that all her friends had parents who cared about them and made them feel good. When it was pointed out that what she had just said meant she must have some friends she would say that they weren't real friends because she knew that they didn't really like her.

Rosie would always have stories that sounded real to demonstrate the fact that no one loved her. She hadn't got anywhere to go on a Saturday night or she hadn't been invited to go to town with a group of girls, or her parents didn't ask her what had happened at school that day. In the end she complained so much that she drove everyone away. What she had believed was happening had come true.

Rosie didn't realize that she had pushed people away so far that no one dared to invite her out or would risk being interested in a part of her life because she could be so nasty back to them. She was dismissive of their interest and efforts.

Rosie was her own worst enemy. She was like a snapping crocodile that only wants to be stroked but doesn't know how to stop snapping. People gave Rosie a wide berth, so there was the truth, in Rosie's eyes, that nobody loved her.

When she got upset about nobody liking her Rosie would start to take risks. 'If nobody likes me I might as well . . .'

On a bad day Rosie really didn't

- like or care for herself;
- like or care for anyone else;

- know how to accept help;
- think she was worth anything.

On a good day Rosie was

- affectionate
- good fun
- efficient
- able to enjoy other people's company.

Rosie's predicament

Rosie didn't look after herself at all. She seemed to think that it was other people's job to find some way to live her life for her.

Rosie needed to understand that her life was her responsibility. She was the most important person she had to care for. She didn't have to persuade other people to like her. She had to like herself. She simply had to find a way of life that she felt she could manage.

She would know she was managing her life if she could:

- enjoy the day without feeling let down;
- recognize when she did something that made her happy;
- enjoy her own company;
- realize that success was everywhere and hers for the taking;
- know she didn't need to compete with her friends.

Rosie needed to know that it was all right for her to feel happy now she was older although she had felt very unhappy when she was younger.

Until Rosie got a sense of what she was worth to herself other people's efforts would always feel disappointing to her.

Being yourself

When children are very young they rely on their parents to make sure they can cope in public life. They have to learn the subtle requirements in each situation they find themselves in. Very young children seem to be confident of their path and two-year-old tantrums have a lot to do with defending their path. When teenagers are knocked off their path, as they can be by events in their lives, adults need to show them how to find their way again.

The important thing to remember is that we all have to deal with our own world. We can do things with other people but we must respect that they are different and so are we.

It is liberating for teenagers and adults to realize that they:

- don't have to be liked by everybody;
- don't have to like everybody;
- don't have to like people that other people like;
- don't have to make judgments about other people just because they are different;
- can have a friend and not like everything about them;
- can have friends who don't like everything about them;
- don't have to be perfect.

Life does not have to be:

- a series of personality contests
- predictable
- fair
- always going to be the same as it is now.

When you know that you can mix with people without liking them your social circle will expand. It will include people with the same interests as you, whom you call friends, although you will limit what you do with them to your shared interest.

When you know you can be interested in people without them liking you you can learn from them. When you know you can take pleasure in your strength in social situations you can be comfortable wherever you are. You are confident to leave places if you don't like them, without making other people feel unhappy.

When you know people can be interested in you without them liking you you will feel happy to tell them what you know and to talk about what they are interested in.

When you know people can like you but not have a lot of time to spend with you you can really look forward to the time you will spend with them and have a warm, fuzzy feeling inside when you think about them.

When you know that whether you like somebody or not you can do things together, you can be a fan without being a friend.

When you know you do not have to compete with everyone you meet you can relax in company.

When you know everyone you meet is not competing with you you can enjoy listening to whatever they have to say.

If you can do any of the above you will be able to accept offers of help, accept offers of friendship and see opportunities for company that are available.

If you think that life is all about personalities and perfection you will either be on an emotional roller-coaster or in an emotional desert. Being detached about friendships doesn't mean being remote.

Any long-term relationship depends on the people in it knowing how to cope with the bits they don't like. In the world that young people are experiencing there seems to be no place for imperfections. If someone doesn't measure up in all areas then many teenagers seem to feel they need to be dismissed. If a teenager dismisses everyone around them they will not know how much they have lost.

Remember

- Hormones affect teenagers.
- Violent swings in emotions and reactions are common.
- The emotional upheaval doesn't disappear when the teen age is over unless teenagers are helped to manage their emotions.

Teenagers who dismiss offers of friendship

Andy was always withdrawn. He wasn't interested in other people. He wasn't interested in doing anything with anyone else. He didn't like schoolwork and he didn't like school.

He made it impossible for anyone to break through the barrier he had put up.

Reeta had impossibly high standards. She was skilled at computers, interested in science, brilliant at debating and wanted to be an actress. She had no time for the people at her school and felt it was a waste of time to try and make friends outside school. Because she felt superior she didn't join the local drama group even when her mum's friend asked her to. They put on musicals and pantomimes that she felt were way below the standard where she wanted to be.

Terry snarled at everybody. Since his best friend had moved house when he was six he had decided that he wouldn't trust anybody. He also decided that he wasn't worth liking. If anyone tried to make friends with him he belittled them. He felt anyone who would want to like him must be a totally inadequate human being.

Some teenagers who dismiss offers of friendship don't feel worthy of being a friend or that anyone is worthy enough to be their friend. They have such a low opinion of themselves that if anyone tries to be their friend they see that person as being desperate. Why else would they want to befriend the teenager who's such a loser? Other teenagers shy away from the rough and tumble of making friendships because they feel too scared. Some teenagers feel they don't fit in and accept that they are different.

How to help teenagers who dismiss offers of friendship

- See if you can arrange family things where other teenagers of the same age are invited.
- Encourage them to join in with groups of all ages. There are many opportunities for teenagers to feel part of something without suffering the agonies of feeling they are not good enough.
- Belonging to things like orchestras or sports clubs can be a way of being around young people of the same age while having something to do so they are not forced to make friends. Belonging to a postal fan club where newsletters are sent out can help some teenagers feel as if they are in the swim.

Teenagers who dismiss offers of support

Hannah had a strong sense of her own identity and her need to let others know that she could cope. If anyone offered her any assistance – a sewing machine to speed up her job of making costumes for the school play or a lift into town to save her catching the bus on a wet day, or their notes when she had been away – Hannah would refuse. She felt that any help taken would show her to be someone who couldn't do it herself. In her mind, accepting help was the beginning of a slippery slope away from self-sufficiency.

Cheryl dared not take help. She was desperate to be the same as everyone else. If all her friends went somewhere Cheryl had to go. If all her friends wore a designer label so did Cheryl. Cheryl never made a decision for herself. She watched her friends carefully and made sure they would know she was loyal. When Cheryl was offered the chance to go to America with her aunt she didn't go because she didn't dare to be different. Her friends weren't going so how could she. When her English teacher offered to help Cheryl once a week to improve her essay writing Cheryl refused saying she did not want to be different. She ignored the obvious differences between her and her friends and clung to the similarities.

How to help teenagers who dismiss offers of support
Teenagers are notorious for appearing to take no notice of their parents' offers of support. However, many teenagers will listen to adults who are not their parents. It can be heartbreaking for parents to discover their teenagers are making strong relationships with other adults. They take advice or pick up on lifestyle options from other people when they won't from their own parents. This is an important stage on the journey to adulthood. If you are feeling hurt that your teenager isn't turning to you then remember how you have decided to look after yourself when you are feeling unsure. Talk to a friend. Let the hurt out someway. You are not strange. You are miserable.

If you are worried that your teenagers are not asking anybody at all, the most important thing is to let them know you love them.

You can't solve everything but if they know that they have your concern and your love they know there is someone on their side.

You can explain that:

- You don't know how to help but you are there for them.
- There are people whose job it is to talk to teenagers. The reason those jobs exist is that everyone knows how hard it is when you are a teenager and you are feeling insecure to talk to the people close to you. You would be happy for them to go to an outside agency to talk to a stranger.
- You would be happy for them to talk to a friend.

Teenagers who jeopardize their future because they want friends now

Tim didn't realize that the choices he was making could affect his future. He wanted to be a pilot but couldn't understand that if he got low exam passes that wouldn't be possible. His best friend thought messing about in class was a good way of passing the time. He and Tim thought up different schemes to wreck lessons they decided were a waste of time.

How to help teenagers who jeopardize their future because they want friends now

Teenagers who are desperate to have friends and keep hold of them often don't have a very clear idea of who they are themselves. They only feel visible to themselves if there is somebody else there.

Teenagers like this need to know that when they do find something that really interests them they will find friends there as well. More importantly they will start to enjoy being the person they are and not need someone else to make them feel a person at all.

As adults we know the value of positive qualities and qualifications. Many teenagers also know this. Some don't. You can point out to them that if they want to choose what they do when they leave school they have to show proof that they can already do something.

You don't have to have a position on the friends that they have got now but you do need to keep reminding them that they will want to choose what they want to do and also be one of the ones chosen to do what they want to do.

9

Rejection

The teenage years are a time when teenagers are desperate to be accepted by the world. They want to be accepted as possible, viable and effective adults. This desire to be accepted can make teenagers feel vulnerable on many fronts. Rejection can come from many quarters and for many teenagers rejection seems easier to obtain than approval.

Rejected by friends

Teenagers can feel rejected because:

- they lose a boyfriend or girlfriend;
- they lose a friend;
- they do not get a boyfriend or girlfriend;
- they do not have a special friend;
- their friend finds another friend;
- they do not have the same clothes as their friends;
- they are not allowed to go to the same places as their friends;
- their house is not the same as their friends';
- they do not look like their friends.

When teenagers feel vulnerable they feel unsure.

Vulnerable

Adam had been ill and he had become very thin. He was hoping he would build up his body again but although he ate all the time he couldn't put on any weight. His friends had girlfriends but he didn't. He was sure it was because of his skinniness. He felt vulnerable.

Betrayal

Vicky's friend Jenny phoned Vicky and said that she wouldn't be able to go out with her on Friday as they normally did because she had so much work to do. Vicky accepted what Jenny said and went out herself with some other friends. She felt completely taken for a ride when she saw her boyfriend and Jenny coming out of a cinema later on Friday evening. Her world fell apart and she felt a fool. She had to cope with overwhelming feelings of betrayal.

What you can do if your teenager feels rejected by friends

First, do not despair. Being rejected sometimes is not the end of the world. Your teenager is not going to be friendless for ever. Second, talk about the feelings people have when friends move in different directions. Sometimes the rejection can be two-way. Teenagers can feel confused by the fact that friends they liked before are changing or they themselves are changing. The old friends cannot be the same companions they were.

The pain when teenagers lose friends can be greater than any pain they have experienced so far. They can feel lost, unsure, fearful, sad. The stress for somebody who wants to change a friend can be more acute than any stress they have felt so far. The stress of breaking up a friendship can be followed by a sense of freedom and relief.

The third thing you can do if your teenager feels rejected by friends is to explain that if they say or do nasty things to their ex-friends they may not feel any better. Comfort them by saying lots of people change friends at different times in their lives.

Finally, suggest they write down a list of things they will be able to do now that they are not with those friends. When one door shuts another will open.

Rejected by parents

Teenagers can feel rejected when

- a parent is ill;
- a parent leaves home;
- a parent starts a new business or starts a new job;
- a parent works hours that are different to the teenager's school hours;
- their parents seem strange to their friends;
- their parents have new partners.

Resentment

Matthew was surprised when his mum said she was going to look for a job. He wasn't particularly interested. He didn't expect that it would make much difference to him. When his mum said she couldn't pick him up from some of his activities he was a bit disconcerted, but there was always someone else who could give him a lift home. When the cricket season finished Matthew was getting home earlier from school and so had a couple of hours on his own before either of his parents got back. Matthew felt the house was quiet and empty. He felt as though something very important had gone for ever. He felt resentful that his world had been changed. He was upset but he didn't feel he could tell anyone.

What you can do to help a teenager who feels rejected by their parents

When there are changes to the domestic situation teenagers can feel put out. It is natural.

They need a chance to talk about how they feel when life

changes. There are going to be many changes now they are leaving childhood and you can help them deal with change.

Write down the changes they are looking forward to, and what you will be doing when they are changing.

Rejected by circumstances

Teenagers can feel rejected if:

- they are not picked for a team;
- they are not picked for some special part in some special event;
- they are moved down groups for some subject or activity;
- they are not as good as others at an activity they have chosen to do.

Useless

Pat had always played volleyball. She wasn't the best but she was a good team member and she was in the first team. Her team got through to the county quarter-finals and excitement was mounting. They won their quarter-final. Pat knew she hadn't played very well. Before the semi-final a girl who had just come to the school joined in the volleyball training. She was good, very good. Pat was devastated when the PE teacher said that the new girl would be in the team for the semi-finals. She felt humiliated and useless.

What you can do to help a teenager who feels rejected by circumstances

Teenagers can feel marked as hopeless when there is a public rejection. They need help to realize that people will be selected by merit in lots of situations. They need to decide whether they want to join in helping even if they can't be doing what they were doing before. They may decide to change course and develop another interest or another skill. It is freeing to learn how to see new positive possibilities. It has to be better than being overwhelmed by losing one.

Rejected by the family

Teenagers can feel rejected by:

- a brother or sister leaving home;
- a brother or sister wanting to have their own life separate to the family;
- the feeling that another sibling is being preferred over them.

Pain

Phillip hated living at home. All his life his parents had told him that although they loved him as much as his sister they didn't expect him to do as well at school. Whenever they went out people always asked Phillip's sister how she was getting on and she had lots to say. When they asked Phillip he couldn't think of anything to say and neither could anyone else in the family. Phillip looked forward to the day he would be able to leave home and live without this endless feeling of rejection and pain.

Teenagers can feel vulnerable if they think their parents only value one particular way of behaving or achieving. Sometimes it is only one parent who has a skewed way of looking at the world. Sometimes it is both. Sometimes it is more in the teenager's mind than what is really happening.

What you can do to help a teenager who has been rejected by their family

- You can get the teenager to think about what they are good at.
- Ask them what they think they need to do to be successful.
- Work out what they would need to achieve that.
- Explain that life is a long game. You don't have to be in the winning position all the time. You can prepare for some future challenge.
- Let them know that the world needs everyone to add to the colour.

- Explain that parents sometimes have limited horizons and don't realize all the opportunities that are available.

Teenagers and stress

Expectations that things will always go right or stay the same can be dangerous.

Teenagers will have to cope with change. They will meet disappointments as things change. Some will respond by seeing other opportunities they can take, others will feel that there is no hope for them. The cost of not knowing how to deal with the changes that happen, and the disappointment that can result, is stress.

Many parents feel that it is dangerous for their teenagers to be stressed and are unsure what to do when this happens. They feel they should be protecting their teenagers from stress.

Teenagers who have too few strategies to cope with stress are vulnerable. Stress is part of modern life. Teenagers who don't have strategies to cope with stress have to avoid situations that are uncomfortable. They have to control everything around them in order to cope. They cut themselves off from the world and focus on an internal struggle. Their energy, thoughts and focus are on how to keep control.

Some teenagers who have no strategies for coping with stress put all their energy into hating one aspect of their lives. They might hate a person, a place or something about themselves. Whatever goes wrong in their lives, whatever they haven't done, whoever upsets them, it is all drawn back to the unsatisfactory part of their existence.

Teenagers need ways of dealing with situations where they feel disappointed or where their expectations have been thwarted. To cope with disappointment, teenagers need:

- fall-back positions;
- ways to rationalise;
- ways to reflect and take stock;

- steps to take;
- the knowledge that they will get there in the end.

What teenagers experience when they deal with disappointment

Anger

When teenagers get angry because they feel rejected or disappointed they have two courses of action. They can be angry with other people or they can be angry with themselves.

If they feel angry with other people they will be bad-tempered, uncooperative and sullen. If they feel angry with themselves they can become withdrawn, a danger to themselves or sullen.

Sometimes it is difficult to tell whether teenagers are angry with themselves or someone else. When teenagers are angry with others they sometimes find ways of being reckless with their own safety. They do this as a way of paying back the person who they feel has hurt them. What they are saying is, 'Look what has happened to me because of what you have done.' When people are angry with themselves they are more likely to do something that harms them without drawing any attention to what they are doing. They feel so bad they punish themselves. They don't feel part of what is going on. They withdraw.

Self-doubt

Whether a teenager feels valued or under-valued may not be dependent on the parenting they have received. Some teenagers begin to feel self-doubt without anyone even realizing. They are good at behaving in a way that doesn't arouse suspicions. Sometimes the feelings of self-doubt disappear but sometimes they increase.

Self-doubt arises when the image that teenagers have of themselves or what they think they are able to do is challenged.

Holiday terrors

Ryan was excited when his mum said he could go on an activity holiday for fourteen- to sixteen-year-olds. When Ryan read the brochure he thought abseiling down the cliff face, canoeing across a lake, sleeping rough for two nights and building a tree house would be fantastic.

Before he left home he began to worry. His mum said she would pack some of his favourite biscuits and some dried fruit when he said he was worried he wouldn't get enough to eat. His dad lent him a torch so he would feel safe when he was camping out.

His sister bought him some woolly socks that were specially for walking.

Everything Ryan had said he was worried about someone in his family sorted out for him.

He was still scared but he didn't know how to describe his feelings. In his head he could say what he was worried about but there was no way he could say the things he was thinking to his own family. When he tried to tell his family they had said things like he would be all right, or all the others would be in the same boat, or the instructors would teach him anything he didn't know.

The other things that Ryan felt worried about, like being bullied or not being able to make a friend or always being the one who couldn't do it, were too frightening for him to be able to put into words. Ryan's self-doubt was growing by the minute.

Facing up to the fear of going it alone

It is always important to let your teenagers know that the first time of doing anything can be tricky. When teenagers don't know that, they can believe that they should be able to do anything in a knowledgeable, efficient and cool way. Even adults staying at hotels where the whole ethos is to make everyone feel comfortable from the first moment, can look lost and confused. They aren't sure whether they are in the right place, at the right time, wearing the right clothes.

Feelings run high

When you do something for the first time, do you feel:

excited	sick	unprepared
determined	confused	overwhelmed
terrified	fascinated	inexperienced
all fingers and thumbs	pleased	stupid?

If you acknowledge that these are the feelings you are likely to have, you will probably survive starting something new.

Expect the unexpected

If teenagers' self-image means they think they should always be able to handle a new situation as if they are an old hand, the feelings they have might be:

- Complacency. They may think they are doing the activity well enough and not look to improve their technique, speed or accuracy.
- Terror. They realize that what they thought they could do they actually can't do.
- Irritation. They decide that it is everyone else that is preventing them from doing it well.
- Rejection. Instead of acknowledging that they should have prepared differently they feel as if the activity has rejected them. They feel they will have to avoid any similar activities in the future.

If your teenager is giving up lots of activities he or she may be suffering real doubt. Somehow you need to get them to understand that whenever anyone does something for the first time, the chances of them doing it perfectly, or even very well, compared to someone who has experience, is remote. Not only that, but reasonable people understand that young people need space to learn and advice.

Tell them how it was for you

Sharing anecdotes with your teenagers of times when you have come unstuck can give them an insight into the real world, where sometimes things go well, sometimes they go all right, and sometimes you have to put it down to experience. The important thing to know is that however it turned out the first time that is only the first time. Each time you go back you will be able to build a little more.

Take the terror out of trying something new

Anxiety about new situations can be reduced by:

- taking spare clothes;
- going to the toilet before you start;
- having clothes that fit;
- having a tissue in your pocket;
- eating breakfast;
- taking some spare money;
- taking some telephone numbers in case something goes wrong;
- remembering other times when you were a novice but are now an old hand.

Practical perfectionism

Some people are perfectionists. They enjoy getting it 100 per cent right. If they are realistic perfectionists they know that the chance of getting 100 per cent in any activity is remote. It is okay for your teenagers to strive for 100 per cent as long as they realize that getting less than 100 per cent is not a failure. A mistake provides you with information you can use to do better next time.

Perfectionists who think that anything less than 100 per cent is a failure give themselves terrible stress. They will feel they should be rejected because they haven't been up to the mark.

A healthy perfectionist

John had a complicated piece of A-Level maths homework. He was able to do most of it, with some thought, but he could not work out how to complete the question. He looked through his textbooks. He tried different ways of calculating the answer but still he could not work it out. He took his work in to his teacher and the teacher was able very quickly to explain the aspect John had not realized was important.

John was a healthy perfectionist. He did everything he could do. He put effort into trying to understand what he couldn't do and then he recognized he would need help.

A stressed perfectionist

Fiona was in John's class. She had the same homework. When she tried to do the same question she became angry when she couldn't get the whole answer. She looked through her textbooks. There didn't seem anything there that would help. She sat up all night determined to solve the question. In the morning she was exhausted and distraught. When she went into school it was almost impossible for her to speak to the teacher at all.

Fiona was so keyed up the teacher asked her to come back at lunchtime. Even though the teacher had set aside half an hour to explain how to do the problem, Fiona was so stressed she couldn't take in what he was saying.

Flaring up

Some teenagers fight fear with fire. They have a terrible fear of rejection. They will flare up at any demand that they feel will put them at risk of being rejected.

When Lawrence was asked to read out the part of Toby Belch in his English lesson he refused. He knew that if he had to read that part the others in the class would laugh at him. He insisted forcefully that he couldn't possibly be a character called Toby Belch.

The teacher became angry with the disruption to the lesson.

Lawrence's reaction had now upset the whole class. Lawrence was in a double bind. He hadn't really wanted to upset the teacher so much by saying 'No' but he really couldn't face being ridiculed by the rest of the class if he had said 'Yes'.

How to help a teenager like Lawrence

- Explain that handling one situation badly doesn't mean he will handle every situation badly.
- Ask him if he feels he has let his teacher, his friends or himself down most.
- Say that next time he could try to be braver and he might surprise himself.
- Help him see that he would only be in role when playing a part.
- If his friends do tease him he can count how many times they do it where he can smile with the joke.

Running away

Some teenagers flee the fear. They are so frightened of being rejected that they find ways of avoiding the situation.

Melissa felt the other girls in her class didn't like her. She had spots, she felt she was overweight and somehow or other she just wasn't good enough for them to accept her. The only thing she was confident about was that the teachers thought she was a good pupil. They didn't reject her. She was able to answer the questions. She did her homework. She was respectful and she was able to forget, for brief periods during the school day, that she wasn't friends with the other girls. They knew how to dress, talk and crack jokes. They belonged.

Many teenagers feel like Melissa at some stage. It is a difficult time and it is easy to feel rejected. Most teenagers, when they are feeling like this, muddle on, getting comfort where they can.

Things got worse for Melissa when she moved school. For her it was another world. She felt completely at sea. The first couple of days the girls at the new school were kind, but quite quickly, just like the girls at the old school, they stopped bothering. Worse still, she was now struggling with the work. In Melissa's mind the new teachers didn't like her either. At her old school she felt her teachers had respected her. At her new school they hardly noticed her. At her old school if she put her hand up to answer a question the teachers would give her the chance to shine. At her new school she wasn't picked even though her hand was always up. She was so devastated she stopped going to school.

How to help a teenager like Melissa

On one hand Melissa is being sensible. She is protecting her mental health. She knows that it would be too much for her to cope with to go into school.

- Acknowledge the steps the teenager has taken so far to protect herself.
- Ask her what the benefits are of school. Suggest some benefits yourself. See if there is another way of getting those same benefits.
- A chat with the school where you explain how Melissa feels and ask if they have any suggestions might reveal some possibilities that Melissa hadn't realized were available. She might be able to become a helper or have a mentor that she can discuss her progress with whom she feels wants to listen to what she has to say.

I think I've blown it

Seth was obsessed by football. His biggest dream all through primary school was that he would be able to play for the school team when he got to secondary school. He went to all the practices he could and spent some of each school holiday at a special football school. When the list came round in his first week at secondary school asking for the names of boys who wanted to try for the team he was so excited he could hardly write his name.

At the trial he played brilliantly. He listened and followed the coach's instructions and demonstrated just how well he could play. He was picked for the team and spent the days leading up to the first match telling everyone all the details of his training. His sports bag was ready. He had a photograph taken in his new strip. His grandparents were going to go to the match and he was certain he was going to shine. Nothing could go wrong. He knew he was the strongest member of the team and if the team were to lose then it would be down to the rest of the team not playing as well as him.

In the first five minutes of the game disaster struck. Seth somehow got in the way of the goalie who was trying to stop the ball. In his energetic attempts to get the ball away Seth managed to kick it into his own goal. This had never happened to Seth before. He crumbled and spent the rest of the game feeling as if his legs wouldn't work and the match was never going to end. His grandparents tried yelling their support but all that did for Seth was draw his attention to his failure in front of his family.

These things happen. They often happen just when we thought it was all going smoothly. Seth had put himself in the most vulnerable position by letting people know how good he was and that he would be a heroic player who would be there to support the rest of the team.

The thing about being human is that you can make a mistake. The thing about being human that is wonderful is that you can think. You can reflect on what has happened. You can sometimes work out why it happened. You can plan how you will approach the same situation again and you can learn how to deal with disappointment.

When we think we have blown it we feel:

- embarrassed
- an idiot
- that what has gone before counts for nothing
- shaken to the core
- unable to carry on
- that we have overestimated our true worth and we have left ourselves really exposed
- sick
- guilty
- worthless.

All or even just one of these reactions is enough to make us want to jack it in. Teenagers can feel worse because they haven't had as many experiences as adults of things going wrong.

As an adult when things go wrong you start to remind yourself of the things that you have done well in order to get back into some kind of balance. You may be able to do this for yourself or you may have a friend you can call on who knows just what to say to you when you are feeling hopeless and worthless because you have cocked something up. Eventually as adults many of us are able to turn our catastrophic disasters into humorous stories that even we can laugh at. Sometimes this can happen very quickly, other times it takes longer before we find ourselves regaling our friends with stories of just how badly we performed or just how wrong we got it.

You can put terrible pressure on yourself if you don't learn to laugh about things that have gone wrong.

Laugh it off

Learning to laugh means

- you accept that you are human just like everyone else and you can make mistakes just like everyone else can.
- you accept that, no matter how carefully you plan, something that you can't control may still happen and your plans will be upset.
- being more realistic about your own performance.
- being able to think about adjustments you can make without being too anxious that it will all go wrong again.

Your friends and family will find it easier to listen to what happened if they know that you accept that things go wrong for you in the same way as they go wrong for everybody else.

I'm not laughing . . .

Celia's husband had left her and when things went wrong she would phone her old friend Sally and ask if they could meet for coffee. Sally always dreaded these meetings. She knew that Celia would have tale after tale to tell of the things that had gone wrong. The children's hamsters had escaped and the electricity bill was due. Everything was a disaster to Celia. Sally's attempts to see humour in the situations were met with silence. Sally felt she was doing all she could by listening to Celia. She knew that she didn't have the energy to do any more. Her meetings with Celia left her feeling drained, wanting to lie down and then read something funny to remind herself to see the funny side again.

If you think that you have to take everything seriously or get everything right, then for you something going wrong will always be terrible.

. . . but I am

Jenny was coping on her own with the children after her husband had left. Things went wrong and when they did she phoned Sarah, an ex-neighbour, and asked if she could pop round for a coffee. Sarah looked forward to Jenny's stories. Although they were often serious and worrying Jenny had a way of putting things that soon had them both smiling or giggling uncontrollably. Sarah felt very warm towards Jenny and often offered practical support.

Learning to see the lighter side

Children don't see the irony in situations. It is only as they grow older that they can see the funny side of something quite serious or sad.

In families where parents laugh at their own mistakes children will learn to laugh when something goes wrong. At first they might laugh at their parents' mistakes but feel very sensitive about their own and then they become braver about laughing at their mistakes too.

If you can laugh about things going wrong you have a chance to balance the hurt with a grin. You might not laugh at the time but you can see the funny side later. You tap into another resource that you couldn't draw on at the time.

10

Creating confident teenagers

The world is ready to receive your teenager as a whole person.

The world is ready to cope with your teenager's weaknesses and strengths.

The world is ready for your teenager to take responsibility.

The world is ready for your teenager to make mistakes.

The world is ready to give reasonable support.

The world is ready to give guidance.

The world is ready for your teenager to grow up.

Are you?

How you think about what your teenagers can do will make a big difference to *what* they can do. Your anxieties can become their limitations.

I feel so worried for her ... she's just like me

Jenny's mum took her everywhere she needed to go by car. She felt that, just like her, Jenny couldn't cope with buses. The one time Jenny had tried to get a bus home from school she had been so busy talking to her friends that she missed her stop and had to phone her mum to come and collect her from her friend's house.

A mistake should be an opportunity to learn. Jenny made one mistake.

Jenny's mum could have helped her to find ways to learn to use buses and avoid making the same mistake again. Jenny could have been helped to find several ways of coping with her mistake. Instead, Jenny was stuck, limited to thinking that she needed to get lifts to go where she wanted and limited to believing someone else would always sort the problem out.

Jenny's mum felt apprehensive about Jenny using buses because of her own experiences. She had never been able to get anywhere on time when she had caught buses. She wasn't able to see Jenny as separate from herself so all the difficulties with buses that she had experienced she saw as being part of Jenny's experience too. It didn't matter that Jenny hadn't had her mum's experience, because her mum couldn't see that. So when Jenny made her first mistake her mum saw it as a continuation of all the difficulties she had experienced. Jenny, just like her, couldn't cope with buses. Jenny, just like her, wouldn't learn to cope with buses.

He's not a chip off the old block

When Alan was young he messed around at school and had to get his qualifications in his twenties. When his son Kieran went to school the teachers complained that he never sat still. Alan was quite calm because he had messed around and he had turned out fine.

Kieran's mother felt differently. She wanted Kieran to do well at school. Kieran calmed down and worked until he got to secondary school where he seemed to go off the rails again. Through primary school Kieran had wanted to please his mother. In secondary school he wanted to be like his dad had been.

Kieran was a boy who thought his dad was a hero. As a teenager he wanted to be like his dad had been. Kieran thought his father's tales of skipping off school, hiding people's briefcases and getting caught smoking were very exciting. His dad was quite relaxed about Kieran's antics because he thought his son had been born that way.

He was his son after all. His mum was frustrated because she knew it could be different.

Why do parents limit their offspring?

- Often parents don't acknowledge that the lives their teenagers are leading are quite different to the lives they led.
- Parents don't notice the differences between their teenagers and themselves.
- Parents often notice only the similarities.
- Parents are afraid that what they are isn't good enough for their teenagers to be. When they tell other adults that they think their teenager is just like they are they're seeking reassurance. They hope to be told that they are all right and their teenagers will be all right if they turn out just like them. Parents who need reassurance like this haven't come to terms with who they are and why they are who they are. It is almost as though they think that the difficulties they had as a teenager are genetic, out of their control, will not get any better and will be passed on to their teenagers.

What do teenagers do when they are limited by their parents?

- They may realize that their parents don't notice some things about them so they don't bother with those parts of their lives at home. Outside their home they may be quite different.
- They may believe that they are not capable and they won't try to expand their world because they find it easier to do what their parents expect.

How to make your world bigger so their world will be bigger too

- You need to make your view of the world into one where you can be confident that your teenagers can be independent.
- You need to make your view of the world bigger so that your teenagers are confident they can be independent.

- You need to make your view of the world bigger so you don't miss out on the pleasure of watching your teenagers grow up.

Just stop for a moment and think

- Are there any characteristics you would not want to have passed on to your teenagers?
- Which of your characteristics would you be delighted to find your teenagers have in common with you?
- Which characteristics do you wish you hadn't received from your own parents?
- How are you different to your own parents?
- Have you ever heard other people describe the qualities of your own teenagers in a way that means you can hardly recognize them?
- Have you ever been staggered when you have been away from home at the way your teenager has handled themselves with a maturity you just didn't know was there?

Careful and trustworthy not clumsy and unreliable

Richard's mum thought he was just like her brother. Richard's uncle had always been clumsy and unreliable. At home Richard was encouraged to stay out of the kitchen. He was never expected to do anything to help because anything he did would create a problem. When Richard took a Saturday morning job he was unsure what to do but the boss gave him the chance to get experience. He helped another employee before he had a go on his own. When he did have a go on his own his boss was delighted. He saw Richard as a good worker, careful and trustworthy.

Everyone needs a chance to shine

Have you ever done something that has astounded the people who know you because they didn't think you could? You get the chance to astound others when you assume you can learn and you have a go. Unfortunately those who know us and think that we cannot learn some things often limit us. They will hold even more firmly to this idea if we have made a mistake in the past when we tried to do the same sort of thing.

If you want to make your world bigger, if you want to get out of the rut of thinking your teenager is just like you, stop for a moment and think. Compare the life your teenager is living now to the life you were living twenty or so years ago. More than their genes and your parenting influence your teenagers. Just like the rest of us, they live in a world full of influences:

- other people they meet
- television
- books
- the role models of the time
- places they have been
- the space in which they live
- the technology they use
- the things they have been bought
- the events that have happened in their lives
- the changes in society
- places they can go.

Check what you are doing

If you tell your teenagers that they are just like you, you put a pressure on them to behave the way you did when you were their age.

If your marriage has broken down and you tell your teenager that they are just like your ex-partner you might be putting them under pressure. If you lead your teenager to believe that they are exactly the same as someone else and not themselves, you:

- limit their chances to be what they want to be;
- limit their chance to know the other person as a whole person;
- limit their chance to know who they are.

How you can break the cycle

- Listen to what other people say about your teenager. You might not agree with what they are saying but you will be hearing how your teenager appears to another person.
- Notice when your teenager reacts to something in a different way to the way you did when you were the same age.
- Notice if your teenager doesn't react in the way you expect them to. Do you feel angry or pleased because they are like you, or angry or pleased because they are not like you, or just interested to see how they have reacted.
- Give your teenager the chance to do things that you didn't learn to do. You might need someone else to teach them how to iron if you can't iron, how to manage money if you are always broke at the end of the month, how to make friends if you couldn't do it when you were young. If you value their efforts when they are learning something you can't do and are optimistic about their success you are breaking the cycle.

Think about how you can shift your position, not how you can change everyone else.

Coping with change

Notice how you feel when something changes? Do you feel excited, interested or panic-stricken?

You will give your teenager the chance to learn if you give them the space to change.

When something changes, do you feel:

- Comforted that you know how someone will react and alarmed when someone acts in a way that you are not expecting?
- Comforted to think that someone won't be able to do something and alarmed to find out that they can?
- Comforted to think you can predict when something will go wrong and distressed to find that it goes right?

You can cope with how you feel about change by:

- seeing it as positive;
- seeing it as interesting;
- thinking about all the changes you have coped with;
- not expecting to accommodate to a change overnight. There might be things that you can adapt to quickly but other things will take you some time.

People who expect things to change find change easier to cope with than people who think they know exactly what is going to happen.

Give teenagers positive messages

The biggest barrier to all of us can be ourselves. If we believe we can't, we won't. If we believe we can, we will. Remember:

- Parents who give positive messages have probably been given positive messages themselves in childhood.
- Parents who can help their teenagers realize that their future is in their own hands are giving their teenagers a very positive message.
- Parents who lead their teenagers to believe that when things don't work out the way everybody had hoped it's somebody else's fault or there's nothing that can be done are giving their teenagers the idea they are powerless in the face of the world.
- People who felt powerless when they were teenagers have to work harder to feel confident and positive when they are adults.

How do people cope?

Plenty of people who have had traumatic experiences are confident. Some of these people will be confident by disposition but most will be confident because they have the skills to help them cope with real life.

Encourage your teenagers to be interested in how people cope with their lives successfully. There are plenty of examples, on the

131

television, in teenage magazines, on film and in their schools, of young people determined to break through a barrier and achieve their ambition.

Creating confidence

Confidence comes from knowing:

- learning anything takes time;
- how to ask a question to get information;
- how to say you don't know rather than hiding the fact you don't know;
- making a mistake doesn't mean you are stupid;
- ignorance can be a temporary condition.

Confidence comes from realizing that to be successful you don't have to be:

- loud
- able-bodied
- the cleverest person in the school
- rich
- popular
- good looking
- talented.

To be confident you have to know:

- that what matters to you is important to you but it does not need to be important to anyone else;
- how to recognize all the things you have achieved;
- that you can learn to do more;
- that when things go wrong the situation can still be retrieved. It is not the end of the world.

How to help a teenager develop confidence

Emily had no confidence. She always had a reason for why she wasn't getting on with what she had to do. She was convinced that if she had a reason she would be justified in stopping. The habit of finding a reason to stop was so ingrained that even if she had everything she needed in front of her she would still stop.

When writing a report about something she had done she would suddenly stop because she couldn't remember a tiny detail that she felt she had to put in. Nearly every time, the detail she couldn't remember was not vital. What Emily needed to do was ignore the fact that she couldn't remember that particular point and keep going. But instead what she would do was sit staring into space waiting for the piece of information to come back to her. She would refuse to write any more even if it was explained to her that she actually had all the information the teacher needed in her notes and the tiny piece she was trying to recall was unnecessary.

Emily would stop in the middle of her maths homework because she hadn't got her red pen and she had decided that having a red pen was vital to doing her maths. The pen became the only thing she could think about. She didn't actually need the red pen to do the maths and she could borrow or buy a red pen in the morning to do any underlining.

Gently does it

When Emily's parents sat down and explained to her that her problem was she was always looking for a brick wall Emily listened, just enough for a change to begin. Each time from then on, when Emily would find some reason for stopping what she was doing, they would gently remind her that this was a brick wall. Emily liked to see herself as an interesting person full of ideas. Her parents used this to show her that she could find creative solutions when she hit the brick wall.

As young people mature they get the skills to care for themselves. Emily developed the skills to keep herself going.

Making the world a bigger place for a teenager who is panicking

Sarah started secondary school convinced she would be able to work at the same level she had at primary school. Sarah thought that now she had more than one teacher the teachers wouldn't notice if she didn't do enough work. She had always done just enough in primary school to keep herself out of trouble, although her teacher had said that she didn't work hard enough.

When Sarah started secondary school her parents told her she would have to do more but Sarah was sure she was going to be all right. Within the first few weeks, messages from different teachers started to appear in her homework diary. Sarah panicked about these messages and ignored them even though they were reminding her to finish her homework. She just kept doing as much as she had been and hoped the messages would stop.

Sarah's parents were asked to go to a meeting at school. They were left in no doubt that the amount of work Sarah was doing would not be tolerated. Sarah was to have a daily report so that her parents would know day by day whether her effort was sufficient. Sarah seemed to accept that things needed to change but when she got home that evening she was like a different child. She began to throw what could only be described as a temper tantrum. She screamed and sobbed and shouted and slammed around. She told her parents that she hated them and she knew they didn't love her. As she stormed off to bed she told her parents she was not going to school the next day.

Sarah's parents were stunned. Sarah had never spoken to them like that before. They were sure that by the following morning, after a good sleep, she would get up as normal. They decided that, in the morning, they would behave as usual and not mention the outburst. They were determined to support the school and make sure that Sarah did more work. Their plans fell apart when, in the morning, Sarah refused to get out of bed. Both parents tried to get her to get out of bed and get ready for school. They used everything they could think of to try to persuade her. Sarah still refused to budge. Her parents were completely baffled. Her dad needed to go to work and her mum tried again. When it was time for her mum to go to work she rang Sarah's grandma and told her what had happened. Between them they decided the best thing to do was to leave Sarah for today. Her grandma had to pop in with some shopping anyway during the day and the cleaner was coming, so Sarah would not be left alone all day.

Everyone felt pretty sure that now Sarah had made a fuss she would come around and be back in school the next day. Her dad rang up the school to say she wasn't feeling very well and she was staying home that day.

Panic doesn't have to be perilous

Most parents have experienced blips in their teenager's way of dealing with the world. Usually these blips are just irritating, but sometimes they become more serious. Mostly parents don't know which is which. It is impossible to know which incident is the beginning of a series of difficult situations that will need to be dealt with quite differently from a blip. If parents get too close and forget they are adults then problems can develop.

If parents can stand back, so they have created some distance and see what happens next, they will be able to decide what they need to do next.

Every teenager who refuses to eat one meal is not on day one of anorexia. All teenagers who shout at their parents are not about to go out of control. It is not easy to be a teenager and it is not easy to be a teenager's parent. It is important for parents to be observant and thoughtful and it is essential that parents do not overreact. The line between doing too much and not enough is blurred. What every parent has to come to terms with is that he or she can only do the best possible and hope.

What Sarah's parents did next

When Sarah's parents came home they let her know they would talk to her about school after they had eaten. Sarah stayed in her room while they ate. Over dinner Sarah's parents thought about what might be happening. Sarah's mum felt that perhaps Sarah was panicking about falling behind and coming to the attention of so many teachers. Her dad felt she was just running away.

They thought about all their options. They could use a bribe. They were sure buying her something would be a disaster because she might think that if she behaved badly she would always get a present.

They realized that going back to school and facing up to the consequences of what she had done was what had overwhelmed Sarah. They knew that they had to help her know that coping with a problem in your life is a grown-up thing to do. If she could show that she was growing up then at the weekend they would have a family night with pizza, music and a video.

When Sarah's parents talked to her they explained what they wanted and Sarah agreed. They sat and watched some television together. Just before she went to bed Sarah told her parents she did not feel as frightened as she had felt the night before. Last night she had thought they did not know how she felt and she wasn't sure whether she could do all the things the school wanted her to do. Sarah's parents assured her that they would be thinking about her. They were hoping that she would see she had learned something that would help her all through her life. They told her that the teachers would be delighted with every bit of progress she made. No one would expect her to be perfect but they would expect her to be trying and making progress.

Sarah went to bed and in the morning before she left for school she had a chat to her mum about one thing she could do so the teachers would know she was trying to change.

Sarah's parents were surprised that she was so confident so quickly.

It is crucial that parents realize that teenagers need support in all their activities. Teenagers can seem to sail through situations but their confidence can be knocked when their predictions are wrong. Teenagers love to know that their parents are on their side. This does not mean that the parents always need to be in agreement with their offspring. It does mean that the parents care.

Caring parents

Parents show they care by:

- being pleased with their teenagers' successes;
- recognizing the effort that the teenagers may have made;
- acknowledging they are growing up;
- sympathizing when they come unstuck;
- being constructive about what they might do next;
- seeing disappointments as part of growing up;
- building on something positive that happened even if overall the piece of work or the activity didn't work out or wasn't the standard that everyone wanted.

Sometimes parents' efforts are brutally rejected by teenagers and many parents feel uncomfortable when their teenagers make them feel like old fogeys. Other times the teenagers are unbelievably grateful.

It is always worth making the effort.

How the media manipulates family life

The media often shows parents and teenagers as stereotypes. Teenagers and parents on television often have only one way of reacting to a situation – to lock horns in a classic grown-up versus teenager confrontation. Teenagers are dreadful and parents are long-suffering. This is not the only truth. Teenagers and their parents are interesting individuals who have many ways of reacting and want to feel loved by each other.

Try not to believe the press when they say, 'You've got a teenager, you've got a problem'.

Parents are preyed on by a media which wants to sell a simple message. The usual message is that teenagers are difficult and no one in their right minds would want anything to do with them. Tragically this means that all the other aspects of teenagers, as a group or as individuals, are overlooked or misread. Parents and teenagers are victims of the message to the masses if they uncritically accept the hype about young people and family life.

When teenagers appear in the media it is because they are in trouble or troubled. These stories are one-dimensional. The teenagers' positive qualities and achievements are overlooked and all that is paraded are their troubles. It is as if the only people who find life difficult are teenagers. The stories ignore the realities of the teenage years. Teenagers suffer from these stories because they feel that they are only interesting if they are in trouble or troubled. Parents can suffer from these stories because they start to believe that every small difficulty can be the beginning of a teenage trouble.

Look for the truth

The truth is that teenagers are exploring life, making wrong choices and not always realizing consequences. They:

- have a wonderful sense of humour;
- enjoy being helpful if they are shown how to be;
- sometimes need to learn how to be helpful;
- are amazed at their own abilities;
- are terrified of their weaknesses;
- yearn to be seen as adult but want the advantages of being a child.

If parents get caught by the media view of teenagers they can miss all the above.

Parents need guidance

Parents who are not sure what they should be doing with their teenagers are in danger of doing nothing. The media often encourages the idea that nothing can be done with teenagers when they go off the rails. It is not easy to help a teenager when things go wrong but it is not impossible by any means.

In times of trouble, the best advice for parents is to think about what is going on. Don't just react to or accept what is happening as the way it is going to be for ever.

Breaking free of the media message

When parents think about what is happening and notice what is going on they can shake off the stereotype. They will be in a position to make changes that will be effective. They will be able to consider whether they want to make a change and how much time and energy they want to devote to making a change.

If parents don't think about what is happening but just panic when something goes wrong they will accept the stereotype. They will look for an instant solution to the problem or decide they have to ignore the problem.

Instant solutions

We are constantly offered instant solutions that will make us feel better. The problem with an instant solution is that it will not address the real reason for the problem. An instant solution is much more likely to be general rather than specific.

Advertisers encourage us to have knee-jerk reactions to all situations. Whoever is advertising a product wants you to buy their product. They make you believe their product will solve your problem. This is fine if the problem is some spilt red wine on a new cream carpet and their product is a stain remover. It is less helpful if the problem is that you think your teenager is taking risks and you are uncertain about how to handle it and the solution advertised is to treat yourself to a bottle of wine, a tranquilizer or a new pair of shoes to make yourself feel momentarily better.

It is not helpful to believe that emotional reactions and relationship difficulties and anxieties about your life can be solved by a product. A product might give you temporary relief or make you feel nurtured for a few minutes, but the challenges of life are ongoing and you can work them out.

If your teenager speaks rudely it does not automatically mean that they hate you and from now on everything they say to you will be foul and make you feel unloved and exploited.

There wasn't enough milk

Harry was constantly irritated when he came home to find there was no milk to put in his coffee. He would fume about it and in the end there would be a shouting match. He would scream at his 16-year-old for being so selfish. When he thought about what was really happening he realized that as a family they weren't buying enough milk and so if the order was increased and some spare milk was kept in the freezer the problem would go.

Harry got out of the trap of thinking that all teenagers are selfish and because he is living with a teenager he will just have to put up with it until the teenager moves out. He decided to look at the problem differently. He realized it was a practical problem that could have a practical solution.

Too often we have an emotional reaction to a practical problem and miss the solution.

Johnnie Applecore

Joanne felt annoyed because Craig always left his apple cores wherever he had been. He ate a lot of apples so there were lots of cores! Joanne felt that his littering of apple cores was an attack on the family home. She tried hard to make the family home a comfortable and pleasant place to be for the whole family. She felt hopeless. Craig seemed to have turned into a teenager with no respect for his home. Joanne tried various things to stop Craig but none of them worked.

During a row between Craig and Joanne a friend remarked that it was a pretty immature thing to do to leave your own rubbish around in other people's space. Craig asked what the rubbish was. It was only the apple cores. Now Craig knew it was just the apple cores. His mum knew that she had probably been overreacting. Craig had felt that his mum moaning about how messy he was had been an attack on his whole personality. He was quite prepared to put the apple cores in the bin. He and his mum agreed that next time there was an argument they would try and look for why the argument was really happening.

He wasn't taking advantage

David asked if he could invite his girlfriend round for tea and he would make it. He spent ages in the kitchen preparing homemade pizza and was delighted when everyone enjoyed the meal. Then he and his girlfriend went out.

When his mum walked into the kitchen she was met by chaos. Food had been spilt. Dishes were everywhere and the sink was full of bowls. She was furious because she didn't have the time to sort the mess out. She felt her son had taken advantage.

As she cleared up she thought about it and realized that the family rule had always been that whoever cooked didn't wash up. What she hadn't realized was that he would make so much mess. She hadn't been taken advantage of. This wasn't the start of her son treating his home like a hotel. She had assumed her son would make about the same amount of mess she did when she made a pizza. She thought about what had happened while she did the clearing up. She saw things she could suggest to her son that would make it easier for whoever was to clear up after him next time. She was pleased that she hadn't had a knee-jerk reaction and launched into a tirade of abuse.

11

Where to draw the line

You can't protect your teenagers from every situation that life presents, but you can prepare them. They may never take your advice, but at least they have it. Sometimes parents are frightened of giving advice because they are frightened of being ridiculed by their children. Teenagers see it as part of their growing up to challenge or dismiss parental advice. Underneath they recognize the benefit of having more to draw on than their friends whose parents offer no ideas on how to cope.

Alcohol

In many families alcohol is considered to be dangerous or not part of family life. Children still hear about the dangers of alcohol but parents don't feel it is part of their parenting to give them alcohol. They see it as just like any other drug and don't allow it in the house. The dangers of alcohol are discussed.

There are other families where the parents drink but have rules that their children are not allowed to drink at home until they are old enough to buy alcohol for themselves. No other child visiting is allowed a drink either. The parents, however, discuss the pleasure to be had from enjoying a drink. They talk about what drinks people choose for different situations so that the children have some ideas for when they are old enough to buy alcohol. The children choose the non-alcoholic drinks they will have as well. There is no particular expectation that when people are adult they will choose to drink alcohol.

Many other families feel that the place for children to learn about alcohol sensibly by trying it is at home where they are supervised.

Alcohol at home with the family

From an early age Tom and his sister were introduced to continental drinking. Tom's parents brought them up to behave in a mature way around alcohol, wherever they might be. They felt it was very important that they should teach their children how to cope with alcohol because alcohol is available in many social situations.

Tom's parents felt that drinking alcohol should mostly happen with food. The children would have wine mixed with water in a wine glass on a Sunday with the roast dinner or for other special meals. There was always a jug of water on the table and water glasses. The children were encouraged to sip their drink and make it last through the meal and to have water to quench their thirst.

Alcohol at home with friends

Greg's mum was very worried about fighting, theft, drug taking and the risks that young people are open to if they go out clubbing. Greg was fifteen and anxious to show his mates that he was growing up. His mum knew he wasn't streetwise. She decided she would need to supervise him while he was learning about alcohol. She said he could have a few mates round and during the evening they could have a few cans of lager. She would get some pizzas so that they weren't having a drink on an empty stomach.

These nights became a regular occurrence. In the beginning she was always around somewhere, but as she became confident that the young people were handling the evenings sensibly she would go out to friends nearby. On these nights she might pop back every so often and check they were all right. When she felt she could trust that the lads would be all right she would come back at the end of her evening and go to bed. The boys might be up until all hours and they would then either go home or crash out and go home sometime the next day.

Greg and his friends were learning how to deal with each other in a social situation where there was alcohol.

Clubbing

Andrew's mum decided that there was no way she could supervise her teenagers as they started to venture outside the house for their entertainment. She decided that they must know she would not be making a judgment on what they were doing but if they needed her in any way for anything to do with their safety or their health, they could ring her and she would be there. Each of her children knew that if they ran out of money and couldn't get home, if friends went off and left them, or if they had eaten, drunk or taken something that meant they didn't feel well or able to cope, a phone call would mean somebody would be there to give them some support.

Whether alcohol is involved or not, it is important that young people know they can pull out of any social situation they find themselves in as soon as they feel uncomfortable. It is okay to decide they have had enough.

Making your own decisions

Laura was going out to a film with her friends. The film finished at ten past nine and Laura knew she could be back to do a couple of hours of study before she went to bed. She went to the pictures in a friend's car with a couple of other people. After the film the other three decided they wanted to go on to a pub. Laura rang her mum to ask for a lift home and then got on with her studies. She hadn't interfered with her friends' enjoyment of the evening and she hadn't compromised her study plan.

Stay cool

Laura knew what she wanted to do before she went out and stuck to her plan. She hadn't felt that she needed to stay with her friends. When a person chooses to study after a film that doesn't have to be a matter of judgment for anyone. It is simply a matter of choice. Laura wasn't implying that her friends should be studying and they didn't feel that she was being boring.

A very important social skill is to know how to cope with the justifiable right of people to do something different to you, without it becoming a personality issue.

Take care
A teenager who doesn't feel confident when there is a change in a plan may not know how to handle the situation if it suddenly changes. They may find that they:

- go along with the suggestion and feel too embarrassed to ring and let their parents know there is a change of plan;
- make the other people feel uncomfortable when they insist on doing what was initially agreed;
- worry that phoning up and asking for a lift home will bring a family argument that they can't face.

What to say
It is a good idea if parents of teenagers try to give them a form of words to cope with possible tricky situations. In this case Laura needed to know how to say goodbye gracefully. She could say, 'Have a nice time and I look forward to hearing all about it tomorrow.' 'Hi Mum, the others are going on somewhere so I can't get a lift home now, would you mind picking me up?'

Safety matters

It is obviously important that no young person is standing around waiting in an unpopulated and unlit area. Teenagers need to know that they must find a place of safety where they can wait if necessary.

Never assume that teenagers will have thought about all the eventualities. At some point, preferably before they go out, talk about places where they could wait if something goes wrong with the arrangements.

What you told them when they were little . . .

When children are very young parents tell them what to do in different situations if they get lost. In a supermarket they tell them to wait by the information desk. At a cinema children may be told to go to the ticket office. At the zoo the rule might be to go to the restaurant. Learning to be safe is an essential skill whatever age. As you get older the number of strategies you need to be safe increases. When children are little we get them to use the Green Cross Code to cross the road, which means they have to be thinking about the dangers around them and using their eyes, ears and brains to make the judgment. Those first skills are life-long skills.

. . . can still be useful now they are big

Teenagers need to be aware of who is picking them up, whose car they will be travelling in, and once they set off which route they are taking. It is alarming how many teenagers of all ages leave all that detail to the person who is picking them up. We all know the feeling of not being able to get somewhere unless we have done the driving.

Know where you are going

If you are driving your teenagers all the time give them the responsibility of giving you the directions. If teenagers don't get practice at working out how to get somewhere they will have no confidence that they can act independently if the situation demands it.

Be in a state to get there

Teenagers are less vulnerable if they know the way home, walk with purpose, have their money ready and sit looking alert.

When young people know they are expected to be in charge of themselves they are more likely to listen to adults when they advise them to be aware of how much they drink or how vulnerable they might make themselves in any other way.

If they get very cold they may feel vulnerable and accept a lift when under other circumstances they wouldn't dream of getting into that car. This means they need to think about taking a coat or finding a warm place to sit while they are waiting for a lift.

If you feel like a taxi driver

If your teenagers ring you and ask for a lift to get home when they could catch a bus or walk, you can decide whether you are going to pick them up or not. Rather than turn up yourself, you can give them alternatives – they could get a bus or walk. This avoids the problem of some teenagers assuming their parents are a taxi service in every situation. It encourages them to think about the possibilities within their capabilities.

I'd rather you were safe

Teenagers don't always know whether they are safe or not. When parents are encouraging them to become independent there is always a risk that the teenager may get into difficulty. This is part of growing up. It is essential your teenagers know that if they have rejected your advice or made a bad decision or had to change their arrangements and got into difficulty they can still call you immediately.

Some families get their teenagers to ring in every hour when they first start going out and they are not at a friend's house. Then they ask them to ring only if there is a change of plan or a difficulty.

Getting it wrong

Parents are human, just like teenagers. While teenagers are growing up parents are learning as well and they will make some good decisions and some decisions they wished they had never made about what they allow their teenagers to do. They need to forgive themselves, just like they need to forgive their offspring.

As long as parents remember that they are learning all the time, mistakes are likely to be corrected before there is a disaster.

Things can go wrong for a variety of reasons. Parents may go along with something or agree to a request because:

- they are anxious to make sure their teenagers get advantages that they never had.
- teenagers tell their parents what they know will put their parents' minds at rest, whether it is true or not.

- they feel that everyone else is allowing their teenagers to do or to have the same.
- they may have decided that the best way to run their own lives is to give in on the things that don't matter and only worry about major issues. The danger of this approach can be that major issues that should be dealt with are ignored because parents mistakenly believe they are trivial issues.

In the same way as young people need strategies to be safe, parents need strategies too.

Twenty practical things parents can do

1. Check newspapers and magazines and websites for current information on sex, drug use, anorexia and depression, drinking and food intolerance, and know that experts have different opinions on most issues.
2. Make sure your teenagers know that being polite when challenged by authority is the best way of handling any situation.
3. Let them know you can't stop them doing anything illegal or detrimental to their health.
4. Teach teenagers that they own their own bodies and so they need to know about health – physical, mental and emotional – especially if they are going to take any risks.
5. Discuss traffic statistics so they know the danger of driving or being driven by an adolescent.
6. Let them know that there is nothing they can't tell you. It might take you a little time to learn enough to help but you love them and you are there to support. They may choose not to tell you things and that is their right. It doesn't necessarily reflect on you as a parent if they choose to keep some things private.
7. Get them help if you can't help.
8. Talk about how you deal with dying.
9. Talk about how you deal with a bad day.
10. Talk about divorce.
11. Talk about unemployment.
12. Accent the positives.

13. Send them on a first-aid course.
14. Tell them about the danger of a criminal record. It may stop them being able to follow a career choice or move to another country.
15. Talk to them about how useful and how popular help-lines are.
16. Encourage your teenagers to take a paid job to gain some independence.
17. Encourage your teenagers to manage their money.
18. Teach them how to find things out.
19. Encourage them to collect wise sayings.
20. Teach them how to say 'No', and mean it and act on it.

Sex

Sex for most people is deeply private. We rarely know what other people are feeling or needing to satisfy their real sexual needs. We know human beings have a sexual nature but how that nature develops will be highly individual depending on experience, information and inclination. Many parents panic about their own responsibility in preparing their teenagers for their sexual lives.

Parents' reactions fall into different categories:

- giving lots of information without any other guidance;
- giving information and guidance;
- giving rules;
- watching every move and hoping that teenagers will wait until they have left home;
- knowing sexual activity is part of life and accepting the likelihood that it will start when teenagers want it to;
- knowing rape and abuse is possible and trying to protect teenagers from that;
- seeing sex as part of a whole range of self-awareness issues. They encourage their teenagers to take a responsible attitude to their own person and own possessions and future.

In just the same way, as parents, you want your teenagers to know you are there to offer support over anything, let them know that should they want any advice or just to have a chat you will be there.

You can rethink your decisions

Life is random and teenagers need to know that adjustments have to be made constantly by everyone to cope with changed circumstances. The older you get the more you will be expected to understand the need to compromise. The older you get the more you will be held responsible for the consequences if you don't compromise.

Some decisions are made on the basis that if things stay the same as they are now a young person will be able to do x. It may not be said at the time that x can only be done if the situation stays the same. If the situation does change then three things can happen:

1. The parents still try to provide x.
2. The parents don't provide x.
3. The parents find a way of compromising with the situation and with the teenager.

Not if he's driving

Jenny and her friend were going to be dropped off at a pop concert by her friend's parents. The pop concert was fifty miles away from where Jenny lived. The girls would be picked up when the concert finished near the venue. Jenny's parents were happy with that and the ticket was bought. Two days before the concert Jenny let it slip that her friend's brother was going to take them. He had just got his licence and Jenny's parents were horrified.

If they had taken option 1 they could go along with the change of plan, worry but hope. If they had taken option 2 they could tell Jenny that there was no way she could go. If they had taken option 3 they could drive the girls to the concert themselves.

We haven't got the money

Helen wanted to go on the skiing trip with the school, and her parents agreed. Two days after the deposit was paid her mum lost her job and the family finances were in a different position. Previously they had operated using Helen's mum's earnings to pay for treats.

If Helen's parents took option 1 they might work out how they could cut down on some essentials so that Helen wouldn't be disappointed. If they took option 2 they might tell Helen that she couldn't go on the trip, and the reason why. If they took option 3 they might decide together with Helen that she find half of the money for the trip and her parents would pay for the rest.

Resources need to be used for something else

Even grandparents, other relatives or friends need to have options about what they will do with their resources. Those options need to be understood by the younger generations. For example, some grandparents always buy the winter coats for their grandchildren. As the grandchildren get older the coats cost more. Option 1 would be to continue to find the money even though that would cause real financial hardship. Option 2 would be to say that they wouldn't buy the coat anymore. Option 3 may be to say how much they were willing to put towards the coat that the teenager wants to have.

It is reasonable for everyone to make decisions about their own resources based on their changing circumstances or changing ideas about what they want to do.

We've made other arrangements

When parents change arrangements teenagers can feel devastated because they are worried about the effect the change will have on their friendships.

Tanya was really excited about a trip to the theme park that her friends had been planning for months. They were going on the first day of the school holidays as a group. A bus was going from their area so they had all planned to pay for the tickets and take money for food once they were there.

Tanya had mentioned the idea to her parents, but as the planning became more organized she hadn't mentioned it again. She hadn't meant to say nothing, it was just one of those things. So when the week before school finished and her parents got out their diaries to organize what was happening over the next few weeks, Tanya told them what she was doing. Her mum said that it wouldn't be possible for Tanya to go because her dad had taken a few days off so they could go as a family to stay with some relations. Tanya was devastated. She couldn't believe that her parents had done this and she felt her world falling apart. The group she was going with was the 'in crowd' and she wanted to stay safe inside that group. She felt that if she didn't go on this outing she would lose out and not be invited to go anywhere else with them. Tanya had been looking forward to the holidays because they were starting off with this day out. She felt that if she went to the theme park she would belong to the group for the entire holidays. Belonging to the 'in crowd' would make the holidays fantastic.

Try to get the balance right

Teenagers are in an unusual position of having almost no responsibilities yet lots of possibilities. Exploring the possibilities is as exhausting for them as it is for anyone else.

Friendships and invitations are fragile. If what you want is to know that you belong and that you have a range of activities where you can have company, then you will be dependent on your friendships.

Tanya's parents, just like other parents, were keen for Tanya to have friends and to have a life full of possibilities. They discussed whether they should change their plans or go without Tanya so that she could do what she wanted. They came to the conclusion that this time Tanya would go with them because they didn't feel she was old enough to be left on her own even though she could have stayed at a friend's. They also knew that the relations they were visiting would enjoy seeing Tanya again. They comforted themselves with the knowledge that:

- life doesn't always go just the way you want;
- one opportunity missed does not mean all opportunities lost;
- there are some things that just have to be done;
- disappointment is part of life.

12

Difficult discussions

There will be times with your teenagers when you feel you have to handle a situation with great care. You might want them to tell you something or to tell them something yourself.

You feel nervous about how you are going to handle the situation because you don't want to:

- jeopardize your relationship with your teenagers;
- frighten them;
- make them vulnerable;
- restrict them;
- give them unhelpful advice;
- lose your temper;
- burst into tears;
- show your ignorance or prejudice.

Ways of handling a situation with care

Before you begin
- Go still – take deep breaths, close your eyes, read a favourite poem.
- Jot down why you want to have a talk, how you are planning on tackling it, what will happen if it goes right and what will happen

154

if it goes wrong and what your fall-back position is. You may not have answers to some of these questions but just thinking about the possibility of them will help you prepare what you are going to say and how you are going to say it.

- Talk it through with someone.
- Think about who else might need to be involved. You may need the other parent to back you up so they will have to know what you are thinking. You will both have to agree on what is going to be said.
- Avoid having a stiff drink or a strong coffee to bolster you up. It may only make you more agitated than you need to be, or less clear headed than you would like to be. You may end up leaving the situation muddled. It is better to have a drink of water before you start.

Ways to begin
- Choose a time when you are unlikely to be interrupted.
- Find a space where you can both be comfortable.
- Explain that you are uncertain about the situation so it will be reasonable for either of you to want a break and to resume the conversation later.
- Explain that you are trying your best to make this situation constructive.
- Explain what your motivation is – you might be concerned about your teenager's safety, their long-term future, their health.
- Explain that you feel it is their right to have the information that you have and what they do with that information is up to them.
- Explain how you see your responsibilities.

Danny was still fooling around at school at fifteen. He refused to do any homework and always had a smart answer for any adult who tried to challenge his behaviour.

His mother had always expected he would go to college or university but as the years went on she realized he wasn't prepared to work for his exams. At different times he talked about going to college for a course or staying on at school to resit his exams. She got the impression from him that he thought there would be somewhere for him to go regardless of how he did at school.

She felt that it was time for her to explain to Danny how she viewed her responsibilities for him. On her own she wrote down what his options were and which of those options she was prepared to support. She talked through her list with Danny. She explained to him that she saw it as her responsibility to provide him with a home, but it was not her responsibility to provide him with money. There were college courses that he could sign up for where he would be paid an allowance. Alternatively he could get a job and have money that way. Because she had made it very clear, Danny now had a framework within which to make his decisions. He clearly knew how his mum saw her role once he was sixteen and what he would have to do according to the choices he made.

Before the conversation Danny felt that the choices he was making now would not have any consequences for the way he wanted to live his life. After the conversation Danny knew he would have to think again.

How to bring the discussion to an end

The most important thing is that you both understand what has been said. A good way to check that you do both understand is to take it in turns to say what has been decided. You could write it down so that there is a record. You might want to both sign that you agree or you both know what the other one is now thinking.

If other people need to know what has happened, agree which one of you is going to tell them, what you are going to say and when you are going to do it.

Ask each other how you feel. This means both of you know that the love you feel for each other is not affected by the discussion. What has changed is what you can expect from each other.

Decide whether you need to get together to talk about it again. If you do feel you need to talk about it again decide when that can happen.

If the discussion has become too exhausting or seems to be going nowhere, take the break you said you might need to take. The break might be five minutes, a day or a week.

Parents aren't superhuman

If you don't feel adequate to deal with the situation after you have 'gone still' don't feel you must force yourself to handle it nonetheless. Don't put yourself under pressure. You might be able to delay having to take some action. You might get someone to help you. Parents can't handle every situation that arises as if they have spent years in training for just this moment.

The truth is, there will be situations that you:

- need time to get to grips with;
- feel too emotional about to be as helpful as you would like to be;
- just don't have the words for;
- want to get some more information about before you take it any further.

I can't do it now

You may not know where to turn but you know you are not the right person at the moment. You may choose to ask someone else to speak to your teenager. Or you might write a letter explaining how you feel and why you can't find the words to help, and keep that letter in a safe place for later. The letter will always be there to show that you were thinking about the situation and you wanted to do your best but although you loved your child you couldn't think how. A third option might be to leave the situation and hope that in the future your teenager will come across someone else who helps them to understand, or will find ways to make sense of the situation himself or herself.

There's no pain like heart pain

Simon adored his father who had left the family two years earlier to go and live with another woman. They had recently had a baby and Simon felt quite worried that his dad might overlook him. His mum did tell Simon that his father would never forget him but she was finding it hard herself to come to terms with the end of her marriage and the new baby.

157

On Simon's birthday there was no card from his dad and Simon was distraught. He stayed in his room and only came out to rush to the door whenever he heard a noise. His mum felt for him but knew she couldn't talk to him about his disappointment because her own grief and anger would come spilling out.

She knew that in this situation she was not the person to talk him through it. Indeed she couldn't think of anyone she knew who would be able to comfort her son. Instead she made him his favourite pizza and asked him which video he would like. They spent a quiet evening together.

Before she went to sleep she wrote him a letter about how she felt about him. She wrote that she was proud of him. She wrote she was sad for him but she knew he was a strong person because he had coped when things hadn't gone the way he wanted. It was a letter about how proud she felt of her son on his birthday when he had had to handle disappointment. She let him know she understood that there is no pain like heart pain.

Being positive and helpful

You might decide you need to have a serious discussion with your teenager about something they are doing that you find a problem. To keep your reactions to your teenagers positive and helpful, and not negative and destructive, you need to stop and think. It doesn't matter if you have lost your temper, burst into tears or made rules that can't be kept, as long as you still keep thinking about why the problem has happened.

Who says?

The problem is likely to have happened because your teenager or you have made an assumption that is incorrect. The problem is unlikely to have happened because you have a nasty, out-of-control alien in your home or your teenager has a useless parent.

Discussions can often end up revolving around who can assume the right to tell a teenager what to do.

Teenagers love to argue about whose responsibility it is to tell them:

- what to do;
- what not to do;
- not to smoke;
- how to eat;
- to go to bed;
- to finish their homework;
- whether they can drink in pubs;
- who they can socialize with;
- where they can socialize;
- how to use their money.

This arguing the toss is part of teenagers realizing that in the end they have to make the decisions about how they run their life. They grow to understand there will always be people who can tell them what they can do. There will also always be people there to tell them what they have to do. Soon they will be dealing with employers, landlords, banks and all the other people who are given responsibility for making and enforcing the rules. Their world is getting bigger, and while you can make the house rules they will be taking responsibility for how they deal with rules in the world outside the home.

The teenage years are the time when young people prepare for the real world. They know their parents will not be there to protect them or able to protect them from the world.

It is a time for them to gain many skills they will need to cope with their position as an adult, in the community, at work and in any domestic arrangement.

How can I stop sounding as though I am criticizing?

Teenagers need instruction rather than criticism but it would be an unusual family situation if there was never a time where at least those on one side felt criticized.

When children are young many parents have a very close relationship with them. They feel confident that their parenting skills are working and they take pride in the sort of children that they have produced. This feeling that the success is because of what the parents have done can create a problem when the child becomes a teenager. The teenager appears to have abandoned all the values the parents felt sure they had instilled in the early years and forgotten all the things their parents thought were important. Parents feel the close relationship has gone. The sense of separation can leave parents feeling betrayed or abandoned. They feel that everything they say comes out as a criticism.

Flying off the handle

One of the trickiest aspects about the teenage years is the volatility. Teenagers can fly off the handle because they hear whatever suggestions their parents are making as a criticism. Parents who are trying to support their offspring find themselves being taken on a roller-coaster ride. One minute they have a teenager eager to hear what they have to say and keen to have their approval and the next minute they have a teenager who shrieks at them that all they ever do is criticize.

What is criticism?

Some criticism can be constructive. Some criticism can be destructive. Parents of teenagers can feel they are giving constructive criticism but the teenager hears it as destructive.

Criticism, however it is meant, has the power to destroy confidence. The confidence might be destroyed in an instant or it might be eroded gradually. The net result is the same.

People who have been criticized sometimes but advised mostly only feel vulnerable while they are being criticized. They can tell the difference between criticism and advice and they feel confident to work out whether the criticism is justified or not.

People who have been criticized all of the time feel vulnerable all of the time too. The most vulnerable will hear most comments as criticism and therefore as a personal attack. They may try and decide that some criticism isn't justified but will be exhausted trying to hold on to their belief in themselves as people.

There will be very few adults who don't feel vulnerable when certain comments are made, because of the unfairness they felt when those comments were made at a time when they felt too powerless to challenge the statements.

Under the spotlight

As young people, teenagers are doing many things for the first time and the chances of them making mistakes are pretty high. Whatever the age when anyone does something for the first time they are more likely to make a mistake than when they are more experienced, have had more practice or have gained more skills. So it stands to reason that teenagers will make more mistakes than adults who have lived longer. Often what the teenager has done, which has caused them to be criticized, was in all innocence. They did not realize that their actions would hurt anyone else physically, emotionally or financially. This problem of increasing opportunities and a lack of awareness means the teenage years can be fraught with difficulties and full of mistakes. The teenager can feel under the spotlight and a target for criticism over everything they do.

Don't cry over spilt milk

Sadia was crying when she got her maths mark. Her important exams were three months away and yet she had only got 20 per cent in this exam preparation piece of homework. Sadia was really shocked because although she had always messed around in the maths lessons she had always managed a good result in her work. People had said she was a natural in maths and Sadia had quite relished this position of not having to try very hard yet still coming out near the top. Sadia had assumed this would happen this time. She was distraught.

Sadia was upset because this was the first time she had not got away with doing too little work. Always before when her parents and teachers had said she wasn't trying hard enough and she could do better her test results had still been very good. But now when Sadia looked at the work she knew she couldn't sort it out herself. She felt powerless. There were so many things there that she realized now she just did not understand. She felt she had wrecked her chances to go on and do what she wanted to do next.

She sat in the classroom trying to stop herself crying. She felt even worse when she heard that some of her friends, whom she thought weren't as good as her at maths, had actually got better marks. She felt stupid and betrayed.

The whole afternoon felt like a nightmare. Sadia couldn't look the teacher in the eye. She couldn't moan with her friends because they had done better than her. She felt a fool. She had no idea what her parents would say but she was pretty sure they wouldn't be very sympathetic. Even if they understood, it would be no use because Sadia felt she had probably ruined her life.

You are not the first person to get something wrong

Sadia had a miserable journey home and she was still very distressed when her mum arrived back from work. She had planned to tell her mum in a quiet voice and just show her the mark, but when she opened her mouth to speak the words came out in a wail and she began to sob. Her mum was shocked because although it was obvious that Sadia had not been doing enough work, she had done well enough in tests. She was annoyed that her daughter had not listened to the warnings that everyone had tried to give her. They had all said that she would have to do more work if she wanted to do well in her final examination.

Constructive help

Her mum listened while Sadia got all her miseries off her chest. She explained that these upsets help us do better next time. She explained that as we all leave childhood the lessons we learn can feel quite severe but they can help us move forward much further than we would have if we hadn't experienced them. Sadia's mum avoided repeating any of the suggestions that people had made before.

The way forward

Sadia had learnt that if effort is not put in to a project the results are likely to be disappointing. She could not change the mark on the paper that time but she could improve and try to make sure the next mark was much better. The experience was of benefit because nearly everyone, at some point, learns that consistent success means consistent hard work. If she couldn't improve enough in time for the exam, she could resit.

The way Sadia's mum reacted diffused the situation. She resisted the urge to tell Sadia that this was just what she deserved and they had been telling her that all along. She managed to see this disappointing mark as an opportunity to help Sadia mature.

How to be constructive

If a disappointment happens to your teenager and your teenager wants to improve the situation you can explain that:

- Everyone has to work at growing up.
- Even when teenagers grow up they will still have to work hard at understanding how to do what they need to do.
- There has never been a time when human beings could do everything
- Perfection is not a requirement for survival.
- Most actions do not result in catastrophe.
- Most problems can be resolved or modified as time passes.
- One failure does not mean total failure.
- Every mistake is an opportunity to learn

It is a marker of adulthood when something that goes wrong has in the end to be sorted out by the person to whom it has happened. Other people can offer support but the essential actions have to be done by those directly involved.

Many adults can remember advice given to them through their teenage years. At the time when they were teenagers they probably hardly realized that this advice would be useful and they would remember it at different times throughout the rest of their lives.

When you are a teenager you do really absorb quite a lot although you don't appear to. If parents can remember that and pass on advice gently without criticism they are helping their teenager along the path to adulthood.

You don't love me as much as my brother because I am not as clever as him

Felix was convinced that it wouldn't matter how hard he tried his parents would never love him as much as his brother. His brother was one of those all-rounders, good at school, great at sport and easy to get along with. Felix was none of these. He felt as if when he walked into a room nobody really noticed that he was there. Even at home people hardly ever asked him about what he was doing, but when his brother came in everybody wanted to speak to him. Felix started to lose weight and any interest in life.

Both Felix's parents knew that Felix felt they preferred his brother. It wasn't a new situation but in the past they had been able to find ways to lift his spirits when he felt down. They used to sign him up for a new course that his brother wasn't doing, hoping that this activity would be the one where Felix shone. It never worked, and as Felix got older he wasn't interested in trying anything new.

They did talk to Felix. They tried to explain that he was as important to them as his brother and that he had strengths that would show later on. Felix demanded to know what these strengths were and his parents were stuck for words. Felix told them to go away and he became even more depressed.

Felix's parents were desperate. They went to see a family counsellor. When the counsellor asked them to describe Felix they found that they could only do it in terms of his brother. Felix was tall, but not as tall as his brother. Felix was loving towards his brother. Felix hardly ever went out, but his brother did. Felix didn't eat as much as his brother.

The counsellor then asked them to describe their other son. They did this quite easily. He was a fast runner. He enjoyed school, especially physics. He was good at football and had a fabulous appetite. He was handsome and outgoing with a cheeky grin.

The counsellor asked about Felix's favourite things: his favourite music, TV shows, his favourite type of book, his favourite food. His parents were unsure of the answers. They looked to each other. They were shocked to realize that neither of them knew very much about Felix at all.

The counsellor explained that Felix needed their interest for who he was now, not what he would become. He needed time when the focus of interest was him. His parents needed to find out who he was. They would have to put in some work before they tried to convince Felix that he mattered to them.

Felix's parents needed to:

- try and get over seeing Felix as a shadow of his brother;
- remind each other when they noticed they were falling into the trap of overlooking Felix;
- notice positive differences between Felix and his brother in Felix's favour;
- compliment Felix on something at least once a day;
- ask him about what he was doing, reading, listening to or watching;
- ask Felix for his opinion on things.

How praise makes everything seem better

Praise is necessary for everyone, but especially teenagers. Most teenagers will feel motivated, energized, and focused when they are praised. Praise lets them know that what they are doing is working well in other people's eyes.

Teenagers who do not get praise from adults will be vulnerable if the only praise they look for or get is from their peer group.

Why praise matters

Praise helps everybody feel:

- happy to keep going
- confident they are on the right track
- purposeful
- skilled
- useful
- needed

- noticed
- full of energy
- full of optimism
- like taking a risk to do more.

Praise can help us:

- notice what we have done that has been successful;
- see what we have done through someone else's eyes;
- give value to something we have done.

Without praise we can feel:

- exhausted;
- used;
- taken for granted;
- like we have got it wrong and everyone else has got it right;
- like we have missed some vital piece of information;
- as if it doesn't matter what we do because it will never be good enough;
- pessimistic;
- reluctant to do more than we feel we must.

Teenagers need to know how to get praise

You can get praise if:

- you have had a go;
- you have got it right;
- you have improved on what you did last time;
- you have shown that you have listened;
- you have tried to incorporate what you have been told into what you are doing now;
- you have learnt from your previous efforts.

Take time to praise

The job of a parent is so varied that it is not surprising that parents can forget the importance of regular praise. There is so much to be done that when parents notice something that is helpful they only register it for a second or two before they have to rush on with what else needs doing. They may notice with pleasure that the dishwasher has been emptied which will mean it is easier to get to work on time, but by the end of the day have forgotten what a help it was.

One of the problems about praise is that it is all in the hands of the person giving it. If parents forget to mention what they thought was good, teenagers can think that it wasn't mentioned because it wasn't worthy of praise.

Teenagers are dependent on parents and other adults making it clear when their behaviour is acceptable. It is even better if adults can explain just what it was about the behaviour that they found helpful, mature or pleasing.

Be specific when you praise

The most helpful type of praise is specific. When someone tells you why what you have done is good or better than you have done before you have an idea of what you can do in the future. Their words can help you learn what makes something better.

Steven came home delighted because he had got a high mark for his biology homework. He was stunned because it was the best mark he had ever had. His dad had a look at it with him and asked him why he thought he had got such a good mark. Steven didn't know. He was just pleased he had got it. He thought perhaps it meant the teacher was starting to like him. His dad suggested he ask the teacher why this work was better than other work. The teacher explained that in this piece of work Steven had remembered to use pencil for his diagrams and labelled them all correctly. Steven now knew how he could keep his standard up and knew that there might be other things he could do to get an even higher mark.

Teenagers are embarking on so many new situations and trying to master lots of new skills. Praise that is effective can help them develop and learn. This puts them in control of their efforts. They know what needs more work and what is already working well.

False praise is no use

Praise for something that doesn't deserve praise is not helpful. If teenagers get praised for anything they do they can think that everything they do is something that deserves praise. They think that others should be grateful for any contribution they make regardless of the quality of the contribution or the effort that has gone into it. They don't bother to try and everyone wonders why they aren't motivated.

Undeserved praise

Sometimes it can happen that a person who gives praise goes on to find out something else which means that they want to withdraw the praise. A teacher may have awarded an essay a high mark and then found that it had been copied off the Internet. A teenager can feel mortified when praise gets taken away. The teenager can feel that it wasn't fair. They forget it was their action that led to their feelings of discomfort. They think they have got down-graded just because the teacher is being nasty.

A teenager can also feel that they don't deserve the praise because they know they have got it under false pretences.

Vanessa was very embarrassed when she heard her mother telling a friend how well Vanessa had looked after the next-door neighbour's children. Vanessa knew that she had been on her mobile phone to her friends and had felt fed up for much of the time. She felt she was getting praise she didn't deserve. Like many teenagers, when she felt she had got praise under false pretences she began to panic that people would find out. It was easier to refuse to look after the children next-door again than go through the guilt she felt because she knew she should never have been praised.

Hearing praise

Some young people find it very difficult to hear praise. They may feel so unworthy that they will doubt anyone who thinks that what they have done is any good. We think that listening to criticism is hard but for some teenagers hearing how well they have done can be just as uncomfortable. They would rather hear the negatives about what they do than the positives. Teenagers don't realize that you can get praise even when you are not perfect.

Asking for praise

Teenagers will often pester an adult to praise something they have done, said or chosen. They are behaving like a child much younger, expecting praise for something that doesn't even need comment, let alone praise. If they don't get praised they feel that you don't care about them or that all their efforts are worthless. If you do give them praise they get a false idea of what is expected from somebody of their age.

James was delighted that he had done his homework in record time. He took it to show his father who checked it and found that there were many mistakes. James kept insisting the most important thing was that he had done the work so quickly. He barely listened to any comments that his dad was making because all he wanted to hear was praise for having done it in so short a time.

Transitions like this between childhood and young adulthood can be very trying for all concerned.

Asking about praise

Sometimes teenagers simply accept praise and let it go at that. Sometimes they are so excited about the praise that they want to know more. They don't want the moment of glory to pass so they ask people to give more detail about what makes what they have done so deserving of praise.

An experienced person knows the dangers of doing this. By asking for more details about the praise you can get more than you bargained for. Giving the person or people who have praised you a chance to say more may mean that they also tell you about the aspects of what you did that they didn't feel they could praise. You can go from the high of feeling you can do no wrong to the depths of wondering how you are ever going to have a go at anything again. You learn to be careful how you ask the question in the future.

Teenagers can see things in black and white. Growing up means realizing that the shades of grey in between are worth celebrating.

Giving praise

To be able to praise others for what they have done means that you have to have noticed what they have done. You will be judging what they have done against certain criteria.

- Why are you saying that something is good?
- What have you noticed about what they have done that means you think they deserve praise?
- Will you always praise the same thing or will you keep looking for progress?
- Will something you praised fulsomely last time get the same praise again?

You may be the only person who uses those particular criteria, which makes it even more important that you share your criteria with whoever you are praising.

Coping when you are praised and the others aren't

Getting praise can be a nightmare. Teenagers who are praised can find everyone else in their group rejects them. This is a horrible position to be in because it seems to them they have to make a choice. Either stop doing so well and keep their friends or lose their friends and keep getting praise.

The others in the group can often add to the stress by trying to take their former friend down a peg or two. They may ridicule what has been achieved or how much effort has been put in. They insult the person getting the praise. It can even happen that work is destroyed. All this is done to stop the individual from leaving the group.

If one person works hard then the others in the group who haven't worked hard or done well can feel threatened. If one person in the group sees something as important the others can feel judged as being less valuable. In an effort to make themselves feel all right they can destroy anything that makes them feel unworthy. It can be the root of gentle teasing, unpleasant bullying or vicious attacks.

Teenagers who are suffering the bullying or doing the bullying need help. First they need to realize that they have to find ways of coping. They need to know that when they are older they are going to have to cope with people who choose to be different to them.

Helping the bullied and the bully through praise

- Praise works. Tell them how well you think they are doing. Bullies have low self-esteem and that is why they want to attack the self-esteem of others. Their victims' self-esteem could be low as well.
- Suggest they get help from school if they can't cope. Some schools can sort out bullying problems but not all bullying is easy to correct.
- If no one can help, they will have to help themselves. Show them the chapters in this book that deal with making yourself strong, learning to relax and thinking things through.
- Praise them every time you notice that they are being brave, working on themselves and thinking of a way through.

You can't overcome every problem that your teenagers have but you can help your teenagers overcome their own problems.

13

Teaching teenagers to be content!

Parents often say that they want their teenager to be happy. They don't often specify what they mean when they say that.

Say what you mean

Some parents actually mean that while their teenagers are living with them they are happy if their teenagers are doing what they, as parents, are happy for them to do.

Other parents mean that their teenagers should be happy as often as possible. They believe they should make their teenagers happy and other people should want to make their teenagers happy as well as them.

Still other parents mean that they want their teenagers to be able to choose a wise way of living which will mean they have the ability to look after themselves and their own needs in a way that will make them happy.

Find out what they think you mean

What some teenagers hear is that their parents' main wish is that they are happy all the time. This can lead to many arguments because the teenagers can feel their parents are being unfair if the teenager is feeling less than happy. This can be very limiting for a teenager and very destructive for family, school and social life because the teenager sees happiness as only coming from immediate treats. They see happiness as what someone else should provide for them, not something that they should contribute to.

Teenagers who think like this then claim to need an unending supply of money, patience, possessions, treats or lifts in cars to keep them happy.

If school doesn't make them happy, they don't feel they should go.

If a Saturday job doesn't make them happy they can't see why they should have one.

If hanging around with the local gang and smoking is a laugh, then they feel that is what they should be allowed to do because it makes them happy.

If last month's jacket is out of fashion then they should have a new one because that will keep them happy.

Hype and happiness

The media gives teenagers the message that they only have value if they are buying something. Huge budgets are spent on research and marketing that is directed toward turning young people into customers. Teenagers are very important as consumers. They have surplus money to spend on themselves. If teenagers can be encouraged to see themselves as buyers of CDs, clothes, computer technology and films then the advertisers hope that they will carry on spending on these items as their incomes increase. They will have customers for life.

Teenagers are encouraged by advertisers to see that buying something will make them happy. They will be happiest if they buy the same as all other teenagers. Advertising encourages teenagers to be like everyone else. The media does not give teenagers lessons in how to become individuals.

Don't judge a book by its cover

The implication in advertisements is that if you are a teenager with the right credentials you will want to buy the product that is being advertised.

Teenagers feel convinced by the pressure to spend money to show they are part of the group. They will spend more than they need on designs that are fashionable. They need proof that they are OK. Wearing fashionable clothes with the right labels is the proof. They will want the label so much that they wear it on the outside of their clothes so no one is in any doubt they are someone who knows how to fit in.

Instant happiness

This approach to instant happiness is misplaced. It is under-standable that young people see gifts, phone calls, invitations, feeling they belong, feeling attractive and feeling grown up as fundamental to being happy. They live in a commercial world where messages about how to be happy are linked to what you have. They hear and see all the time examples of people getting things that make them happy, from a new car to a new baby, from a haircut to a holiday, from a new job to a new partner.

Teenagers are encouraged to think that getting 'things' will provide complete happiness. What they don't see is that no 'thing' is as powerful as that. If they believe the marketing that is all around them they think happiness comes easily. Some 'thing' will make you happy. If you haven't got the 'thing' you want then you should be unhappy. If you have got the thing you want you will be happy.

The right to be happy

Teenagers think that happiness comes as a right. They think

happiness has to be seen. They see people who are cheerful, chirpy, delighted, ecstatic, exuberant, elated, enthusiastic, overjoyed and thrilled as happy. They are less likely to recognize that when they see people who are contented, satisfied, calm and have a sense of well-being they may be happy too.

Parents and other adults have to explain that happiness is how you live your life, not necessarily what you have. Happiness has different forms. True happiness is feeling at peace with everything including the person you are. Happiness can be worked towards. Happiness can be learnt.

Teaching teenagers the skills they need to be happy

Teenagers need to be taught the skills to be happy because being able to be happy is a skill and a blessing. If you have the capacity to be happy you will:

- enjoy your life;
- delight in the world;
- add to the enjoyment of other people;
- be content with yourself;
- not be easily bored;
- see opportunities that will sustain your happiness.

How do you see happiness?

If adults see happiness as coming from things that people need to have, rather than things that people need to be, then they have little chance of teaching teenagers what they will need.

If adults see happiness as coming from what people are, rather than what people have, they have a chance of teaching teenagers the basic values that have sustained human beings in the face of the most awful catastrophes since time began.

If teenagers can be content even in the face of disappointment they have survival skills for a happy life. If they can find ways out of a disaster they will have essential skills for a happy life. Disappointments and disasters are a part of everybody's life. We can't protect teenagers from problems or sadness but we can teach them how to see the world in a balanced way.

The future is beyond imagination

Parents who are bringing up children today cannot imagine the demands that may be made of those children when they reach adulthood. For most parents, thinking that far into the future is impossible to do.

When parents think what life skills they have needed they will be able to imagine what life skills their teenagers will need in their own lives. Life skills are all about knowing how to support yourself, how to support others and how to ask for other people's support for the things you have to do. Life skills, once they are learned, become part of us and can be drawn on if we remember they are there.

The life skills you need for happiness

- You can give as well as take.
- You can make a contribution.

Teenagers can think that giving and taking is all about what they can buy or what can be bought for them. Their whole relationship with their parents revolves around what they want their parents to buy them next. Because their vision is so limited they need help to open their horizons and recognize that giving is more than what you get. Carrying a heavy bag for someone, opening a door, giving a smile, being given a lift, making a cup of tea, having a meal cooked and helping tidy the garage are all part of giving. Giving is not only to do with money, and neither is it only one way. It is also:

- noticing when chances arise for you to make a contribution;
- being careful that the contribution you can offer is one you can really make;
- knowing that one of the people you are contributing to is yourself.

Making a contribution can feel great. Letting teenagers make contributions can make them feel great too.

There are crucial life skills that teenagers need to learn so that they can live independent and fulfilling lives as adults. Otherwise they will be tempted to seek instant happiness that can be costly in terms of their money, time, health and future. These skills are

- knowing that there will be good days and bad days;
- knowing that you are capable of learning how to do something that appears quite hard;
- knowing how to organize;
- knowing how to prioritize;
- knowing you can't get everything done;
- noticing what is going on.

Not all of the skills will be learnt while they are teenagers. Some will have been learnt at a younger age and some are acquired as we become adults or move through other key phases in our lives.

How can thinking make teenagers happy?

Teenagers who are prepared to think benefit because they can take more opportunities than those who don't think.

Teenagers who think understand that if they can adjust then people will find more ways to involve them.

Teenagers who think know that there are different levels of happiness.

Teenagers who know they must take time out to think things through quietly will have more strength and understanding.

Studying other people to find out how to cope

Watching how other people handle their lives can be most helpful.

1. Look at how other people are reacting in different situations
Don't criticize or judge how they are reacting. You don't need to. You are adding to your store of knowledge about how differently people can deal with their lives. You are making up your own encyclopedia of life.

The same event can cause different people to behave in totally different ways because they each have a different collection of skills and different experiences. Some people search around for more information to understand why something has gone wrong while others redouble their efforts to get it right in the future. Some see a delay as a chance to catch up on other things they need to do while others use the time to reflect and sit quietly.

2. See if you can spot a thoughtful response.
A thoughtful response is one where you can tell that those involved are learning more.

I can tell you are not thinking

Jackie was a vivacious fifteen years old. She loved life. She liked to be the centre of attention and couldn't bear to miss out on anything. She was hard work for adults because her mind was constantly sifting through all the other places she could be and people she could be with. When she was doing her homework, no matter how much help she was being offered, she would not take it seriously. She didn't see that homework or schoolwork had anything to do with her real life. Her real life was making friends, contacting friends, being with friends and talking about her friends to other friends. No matter how much her parents or teachers talked to her Jackie took not a blind bit of notice and went on in exactly the same way.

At home her demands on her parents were very high. She wanted them to listen to every detail of her life. She was very theatrical and noisy. One demand followed another. Although she wasn't materialistic her priorities were all wrong. Her parents had to keep checking to see if Jackie had done any of the things she was supposed to do. Like many teenagers she was quick to interpret help that she had demanded as intrusion. She wasn't prepared to think about her life at all. She had so little idea that she was supposed to be a student as well as a friend that she made very little progress.

Jackie couldn't make progress because she wouldn't think about any of the suggestions that anybody else made or reasons they gave her for why she should change. She had such a strong picture of what she wanted to do that she couldn't think of anything else. When Jackie got a Saturday job she didn't survive the trial period. In many ways she was relieved because she knew she had done it badly and really didn't know how she could do it any better. She kept muddling things up. She kept thinking the customers were her friends. She didn't realize that she was there to provide a service. When the job had been explained to her she hadn't really been listening so she had no idea what she should be doing. She didn't slow down enough to give herself space to work it out. She had no understanding that in this situation she needed to adjust the way she behaved, look at how other people were behaving and pay attention. She needed to think about what she was doing.

It pays to be thoughtful

The reason adults become concerned when teenagers learn to drive and are given powerful cars is that teenagers often don't know how much thought something takes. For the same reason many adults worry when teenagers become parents. Teenagers are in the very early stages of learning how to think through something that requires concentration and still be aware of the other things they need to do. Even very intelligent, well-behaved, highly achieving teenagers take time to realize that thinking things through matters.

If you have teenagers who are not thoughtful and who rush through everything, even things they should be spending time on, all you can do is be patient and consistent. That is a very good model for your teenager to see. You need to keep an emotional distance so that you are not driven to distraction.

Let your teenagers know that in general the thought put into any activity determines the quality of the outcome. It can take years for some people to realize that if they contribute something of themselves, their thoughts, their actions and their concern, then the experience they have is totally different to the one they get when they don't.

Let them know there are some things that can be done without a great deal of thought. Supermarket shopping can be done while you are thinking about something else, and although you might forget things it won't matter too much. Enough of the job will still be done and it is likely to be done well enough to allow you to keep going. However if you do the same thing about paying your bills you can end up bankrupt. Adulthood requires the ability to recognize the level of concentration and thought necessary for different tasks.

Helping teenagers adjust

Notice how you adjust and control the world around you when you are facing a tricky situation. When you have to make an important phone call do you:

- Go into a room on your own?
- Turn off the TV or the radio?
- Think of the first thing you will say when the phone is answered?
- Have a piece of paper and a pencil handy?
- Have all the information to hand?

When you are reversing into a car-parking space do you:

- Switch off the radio?
- Take off your sunglasses?
- Ask people in the car to watch out?
- Ask people in the car to be quiet while you make the manoeuvre?

When you ask for quiet or stillness say why

Don't assume that your teenagers know how you are thinking

through what you have to do and what you are adjusting to make sure it works. Teenagers who don't know how much thinking their parents do, even when they are doing something that is routine, can think things happen without thought. If they see their parents taking time and care they can think their parents are boring or getting old. They need to know what adjustments you make in terms of your time, your energy and your concentration so that you can drive safely, write a note or sort out some minor domestic crisis.

Teenagers need to think about situations where they have been successful and pleased because they have been thoughtful and made sensible adjustments.

14

Asking for help is okay

You may feel reluctant about asking anybody else for help with a problem in the family. You might feel:

- You are responsible for the problem in some way.
- People will despise you or your teenager for having the problem.
- Other people will find out.

Don't worry. There are plenty of ways of finding out information on almost any subject under the sun, or any problem that parents may have concerning their children. You can find out information from someone face to face or you can get help without anyone knowing who you are.

Seeking help is quite natural. In the past when there were more chances to meet other parents, and people lived in extended families and holidayed nearer home, information was passed through the community. Now parents are more isolated and so a whole range of support agencies and information-providers exists to give specific information. Help is available from a range of places when you have a problem:

the library   television programmes
the doctor   places of worship

the school
a friend
a book
leaflets

self-help groups
the Internet
a counsellor.

When you are looking for help you might know quite clearly what sort of help you want. In that case you will keep going until you find someone or something that suits your need.

You might be hoping that someone else will know the help that you want. In that case you will find someone who can take you through what is available and the options that are open to you.

In the end what happens is that when you have searched for information you will know more about your problem than some of the people providing the information. This is understandable, as you know your own circumstances in addition to the information you have been given.

Remember that just because you have asked a question doesn't mean that the person answering it will give you all the information they have got. They will decide on what they think you are asking for. If you are asking for help you will often get further if you explain your situation. Otherwise the person you are talking to is trying to guess why you want to know. 'I have just heard that my daughter of fifteen is pregnant and she wants to keep the baby, who is the best person for me to talk to?' is a better question than, 'Can you tell me about teenage pregnancy?'

If you are talking to a friend because you need someone to talk to just to try and clear your mind or get some comfort, you don't need to worry about being as clear as you can. Talking to a friend often helps you get your ideas straightened out so that you can ask other people for help.

When talking to teachers it is always a good idea to find out what they can do and what they would like you to do.

If you search through books and on the Internet for help you will gradually pick up keywords. Keywords are the words that keep appearing in articles. They may be up-to-date words for things you know about but call something else. If the language used by experts baffles you, ask them what they mean. You can build up a list of keywords and their meaning so that you don't feel at a loss when experts are talking to you. You may find that experts use the same words to mean different things. If you are speaking to an expert and you don't understand what they are saying don't feel a fool. Tell them what you have understood and ask them to explain the bit that you haven't understood again. Then the expert will know where to start with the explanation and you won't have to sit through more explanations for something you already understand.

Many people find self-help groups useful because they like to hear from people who have first-hand experience of what they are going through. Some people prefer the flexibility of looking where they want to for an answer and feel they might be inhibited if they joined a group.

If you are looking for spiritual help that will give you strength and comfort, places of worship often have facilities to put you in touch with someone who can listen or someone who can give you practical help.

There is a huge amount of information available through the media and some of it will be just what you want when you want it. However, there can be few people who aren't aware that the media can give information that is more confusing than helpful. You can go in search of a remedy or a service that you have read about in the paper and find that it doesn't have the capacity to deal with general enquiries. Don't give up if this happens. Look around, there could be something else.

Whenever you go to see someone for help find out whether they have some information that you can take away to look at before you commit yourself any further. Check whether the information and the claims are real from the experience that you have already had. If you have any doubts, don't feel driven by desperation, or by the fact that you read it in the paper or in a book, to keep going. Always keep your wits about you. Some services that are funded by charities have to show that they have helped a certain number of people. As long as they can show they have done something the quality of what they offer may not be consistent.

For a list of helpful organizations, covering a wide range of issues, see the 'Useful addresses' section at the back of the book.

15

Recharging your batteries

When you are feeling stressed, tense or under pressure the temptation can be to:

- take control of everything;
- abandon control completely.

The best thing to do is to take control of yourself and not worry about trying to control everything else.

Techniques for taking control

The best way to take control of yourself is to tune out the static that is causing you distress and tune into the calm that lies within you.

Practise these techniques for taking control of yourself. Then when you are tempted to feel quite frantic about something you will find that you can still keep in control. If you practice even when you are not stressed you will find that you:

- get less stressed when something goes wrong;
- get stressed less often.

Stress comes when you don't have the resources to deal with a problem. You may not have enough time, enough money, enough space to think, enough energy.

Too much to do

When children reach their teenage years you can find yourself really struggling for time. You are at the age when you are:

- young enough to care for older family members;
- old enough to care for the young;
- struggling with work commitments;
- struggling with financial commitments.

It can be exhausting, confusing and dispiriting. It can certainly be stressful.

The world and you

You can't change the world but you can change how you respond to it.

You can't control the world but you can manage the way you react.

You can't create the world you want but you can take charge of how you relate to the one there is.

Common senses: how to focus on your senses

By focusing on your senses one at a time you stay aware of what is going on around you and you are not disturbed by it.

Choose one of the five senses – hearing, touch, sight, taste, smell. The object while you are using your senses is to:

- lower your rate of breathing;
- calm your mind;
- release the tension.

If you do this you will be able to respond in a measured way to whatever is happening in your life. Being measured in your response means you:

- decide how much of your attention is needed;
- block out things that don't matter at the time;
- choose the information you need;
- stay calm;
- go at the pace that you can manage.

If you have chosen to focus on your hearing

Close your eyes and notice what you can hear. Notice the sounds that are closest to you. Notice the sounds that are further away. Let your hearing go out as far as it can.

As you listen you will become aware of how many sounds are around you that you don't notice normally. You may also notice how much silence there is. When you try this exercise you will find that you become calm. You get a sense of peace whether you are hearing sounds or silence.

This may surprise you because if somebody told you about the power of hearing without you finding out about it yourself you wouldn't believe how powerful it is as a calming technique. It is only by doing it yourself that you can realize the power of this exercise. Try it now. You might hear the ticking of the clock, the rumble of traffic outside, the hum of the fridge, the clicking of the timer, the murmur of voices or your breathing.

If you have chosen to focus on touch

You can shut your eyes or do this with your eyes open. The point is to draw your attention to what you can feel. Can you feel the weight of your body on the chair or the weight of your feet on the floor? What do the clothes feel like on your skin? Notice how your hands feel and then notice what your hands feel. Is what you are feeling cool or warm? Is it rough or smooth?

Once again you will be surprised at how the level of tension in you drops, as you become interested in something outside yourself. Tension can come because we imagine we know what is going to happen or what should be happening. By focusing on any sense you are keeping in touch with the world you are living in rather than the world you imagine you are living in, or the world you imagine you should be living in.

If you have chosen to focus on your sight
There are several ways of using your sight to steady yourself.

- You could choose to look at one thing and examine the detail. As you look you will see the contours, the shades, the shapes, and the uses of materials. See the thing you are looking at in relation to the other things around it. Notice its height and width. What other things around it have something to do with it? Rest your gaze and let your mind do what it will with the information that your gaze collects.

- You could let your eyes roam around the space noticing the light, where it falls, what it is falling on and where the shadows are forming. Compare the colours in the space you are in and the shades of those colours. Observe what you can see and where it is in relation to you.

- You can close your eyes and do nothing. Rest your sense of sight. Feel your eyelids as a comforting blanket over your eyes.

- You can close your eyes and then cover your eyes with your hands to see how you can be aware of the light changing even when you have covered your eyes. What else do you see when your eyes are closed? Are your eyelids like a screen on which you see patterns, shapes, colours or pictures?

If you are very preoccupied with what is going on in your mind you can be blind to what is around you. You don't see the richness of what is there.

If you have chosen to focus on your sense of taste

You can close your eyes or not and focus on the taste in your mouth. If you want to, you can take something to eat. Make sure that you are conscious of the taste at each stage. Take time to appreciate each flavour.

In a multi-tasking world the taste of food is frequently missed. Wine tasters are able to tell subtle differences because they have trained themselves to pay attention to the detail of what is happening to their taste buds. The more we eat food on the run, or do something else while we eat, the less chance we have of noticing all the tastes.

If you have chosen to focus on your sense of smell

Close your eyes and you may notice some smells that are very strong – coffee, perfume or flowers. As you turn your head you may find that some smells are stronger. If you have trouble doing this, try it in front of your fridge with the door open!

Aromatherapists study the power of certain smells on the brain. They understand how some scents can calm us down while others are invigorating. Smells are powerful triggers for memory. Smells can help our feeling of well-being. Supermarkets know this.

When to use your senses

The good thing about using your senses to cope with stress is that you can do it anywhere. You can notice the noises around you in the middle of a meeting. You can notice the beauty of a flower in the middle of an argument. You can notice the weight of your body on the chair before going in for an interview. You can catch the familiar smell of a favourite coat as you leave the building. You can train yourself to be aware of the taste in the first bite at an important dinner. See if you can still appreciate the taste by the last mouthful.

You can practise using your senses in a traffic jam or in a queue at the checkout.

Why, why, why

Using your senses to calm yourself down stops you feeling:

- driven by time;
- oppressed by others;
- irritated by demands;
- exasperated by inefficiency;
- ignored by your family;
- overlooked by your colleagues and friends;
- misunderstood by people you care about.

It helps you feel:

- calm
- competent
- confident.

When you are calm, competent and confident you will be more at ease with yourself. You will be able to make clearer judgments because you will see what is really happening. Your thoughts will not be cluttered by what you have imagined might be happening. You will be able to control your emotions.

It is important to be in touch with your emotions but not to be ruled by them.

Get away from it all

Your memory can be a powerful tool for steadying yourself when you are feeling vulnerable. Inside all of us are moments of delight that we can bring into our minds. It could be a favourite place you went to on holiday. It might be having dinner with a friend. It could be the time you spend gardening or painting. It could be being curled up with a book. For some people it might be decorating or cleaning.

Powerful, positive memories are times where you felt at ease with yourself. They are times when you had a sense of involvement but also freedom.

Negative memories are also powerful. They make us feel we are not good at coping with certain situations. We have memories of feeling trapped by demands and expectations.

If you learn how to call up the powerful and positive memories then you have a strong front line of defence against the anxieties that arise if the bad memories undermine you. It takes practice but it is not hard to change your automatic reaction from one where you remember feeling negative to one where you remember feeling positive. You can change from someone who feels pessimistic to someone who feels optimistic.

Quality sleep

If you have trouble sleeping, stilling your mind by using the techniques above will help. When negative thoughts are circling around in your head you can choose to replace them with positive ones.

It is important to realize that by thinking of good things you are not running away from your problems or responsibilities. You are simply keeping your mind open to choosing a positive way of living. Once you have a more positive way of living and your mind is clear you will be able to tackle difficulties with energy, clarity and openness.

Give it time

Often we create tension because we try and fit so much in that we don't give the right amount of time to anything. Jobs we think should take five minutes may take six and that creates a problem if we needed to be doing something else in the one minute that the first job over ran.

It is important to decide how long you have got to do each activity and learn to allocate time for doing all the things that are important. This may mean that you have to leave out things you previously thought you should do.

Choose the right space

Sometimes we cause more stress when we try and do something in the wrong place. We think it will be quicker and it is a better use of time just to get it done wherever. With a more careful choice of place it might take the same time but the activity will have a totally different quality. Writing a letter perched on a stool in the kitchen while the kettle comes to the boil will have a different quality and give us a different sense of achievement to sitting in a quiet room at a table. There is no better or worse in this case, but it is important to notice how place and time can influence the quality of the experience and your effort.

Work it out

When you have a problem, choose an activity that creates a space between you and the problem. The activity needs a rhythm to it, like digging the garden, polishing the car, ironing the clothes or cleaning the windows. There is a sense of satisfaction built into the activity because the rhythm of each movement makes you feel that you and the activity are one.

The harmony comes from giving your attention to the activity. When you are giving attention to the activity you are responding to what needs to be done then and there. Outside events will not interfere because your full attention is on just what you are doing. You are not actively looking for an answer but you know that when you pay full attention to the work in hand something happens that lets you work out the problem. You often have the answer but the clutter of all the other activities stops you seeing it.

Wise words

Many people find it helpful and calming to carry a book of wise words or have a note pad with helpful sayings by the phone. All of us have a spiritual dimension and these sayings feed the spirit. When things are tough it is our spiritual side we turn to to give us strength. If we nurture the spiritual side we find the calm we need to handle the life that comes our way. Some people do this through organized religion and other people find their own way, but all of us need to remember that the spiritual dimension is important and without it we are weakened in our everyday life.

Do a stretch to get release

It has been said that dogs stretch when they wake up because they know that those moments spent stretching could not be used in any better way. A stretch:

- lets the tension go;
- encourages you to breathe deeply;
- reminds you that you have a body;
- encourages you to think about the different bits of your body.

Stretching and stress

You might feel slightly ridiculous if you started to stretch in the middle of a meeting, a social situation, an argument or a film, but the benefits of stretching are always there. You can be a secret stretcher by curling up your toes even if you have your shoes on and then letting them stretch. Clench your hands into tight fists and then let your fingers spread out. Make your legs stiff and then let them relax. You will find other ways to relax your body.

The importance of tightening parts of your body before relaxing them is that you are then conscious of how different you feel when you release them. If you try to relax without tensing yourself first you will not be able to let go of all the tension.

Positive posture

Check how you are standing or sitting. If you are slumped, sit up straighter. If you are not taking in deep enough breaths, sit so that you can. Uncross your legs or your arms. Try and have your feet flat on the floor.

Look in the mirror

If you are feeling miserable don't fall into the trap of letting your looks betray how you feel. Check in a mirror to see how you look to the rest of the world.

You will know you have a tendency to put on clothes that are doing you no favours if you have turned up at something special in clothes you vowed would only be used for doing the gardening or painting the shed. Throw those clothes away.

Check the state of your hands. On a day when you don't feel miserable if you notice your hands are dirty you wash them. If you see you have a broken nail you file it. If your hands look dry and chapped you rub in some cream.

You have to develop habits and checklists to protect yourself when you feel miserable. That is what other people do who have washed their hands or polished their shoes before going out.

Without good habits, on a day when you do feel vulnerable, you won't do anything about your hands. Somehow it doesn't matter that you look worse than everyone else around you. It is not that you don't know that your hands shouldn't be in a mess but since you feel you are not up to the occasion your own messy hands won't matter. Then when you are in the middle of the event your feelings might have changed. You catch sight of your hands and you realize that you have let yourself down once again.

Relaxation recovery

Clearing your mind is known to be a powerful and therapeutic way to recharge your batteries and shrug off many aches and pains. People who practise relaxation find that they can think more clearly, get stressed less often, laugh more frequently, waste less time, and in general live a more harmonious life.

When you first start to relax you need to find a quiet place. You can relax by lying down flat on the floor with your arms by your side or your hands resting gently on your stomach. You can sit on a chair with your feet flat on the floor or put a book under your feet if your feet don't touch the floor. The important thing is that your body is supported, your back is straight and your head is in line with your spine.

You can listen to a tape or you can have somebody read the relaxations from this book. You will find that if you read the stories on the following pages to yourself out loud you will still become relaxed if you have relaxed your body first.

Relaxing your body

A good exercise for relaxing the body is the folllowing:

1. Begin by taking a deep breath in and then letting it go. Try to breathe in through your nose and out through your mouth.
2. Keep your breathing steady.
3. Tighten your toes, just curl them up and then let them relax.
4. Tighten your feet and let them go.
5. Make your legs stiff and then let them go loose.
6. Tighten your bottom. Squeeze it together and then let it go.
7. Tighten your back and then let the muscles relax.
8. Pull your stomach in as tight as you can and then let it go.
9. Tighten your chest and let it go.
10. Squeeze your hands into two tight fists. Hold them clenched for a few seconds and then let your hands go. Stretch your fingers and then let them relax.
11. Make your arms go stiff and then release them.
12. Hunch your shoulders up to your ears and then let them drop down.
13. Scrunch your face up and then let your face relax.
14. Finally lift your eyebrows up into your hairline and then let them drop.

By relaxing each part of your body in sequence you can get rid of a lot of tension. If you just try to relax the whole body in one go you may miss areas where you hold tension. Some people have tight shoulders while others hold their tension in their jaw. Some people clench their fists without realizing it while others can keep their legs very tense.

A relaxation for feeling cared about

Imagine that you are sitting by a river as the day draws to a close. It is a warm evening and you are watching the sky as the sun sets. In the gloom you see a tiny dot of light that seems to be floating down the river. It is too small to be a proper boat and as it comes closer you see that it is a little paper boat holding a candle. You look further up the river and see other pinpoints of light. As they float past you see they are all night-light candles being carried in little paper boats. As you watch, one of the little boats breaks off from the others and drifts across to where you are sitting on the bank. It stops in the reeds just beyond your feet. You bend down and pick it up out of the water. Holding the candle in one hand you turn your attention to the paper that the boat has been folded from. You can see that there is writing on the paper. You unfold the boat and find a message that has been written just for you. This is a message that has been sent to you by someone who cares about you very much. They have been thinking of you and have used this river of thoughts and messages to let you know that you are in their mind. As you read the message you feel loved and cared about.

The amazing thing about this river is that it can carry messages from people that are a very long way away, in space as well as in time. Once you have finished reading the message you look down at the river and find a few more little boats caught in the reeds. They are all carrying messages for you and just waiting there for you to look at them. Picture yourself for a moment or two sitting in the warm twilight reading your special messages by the light of those little candles. Feel the calm spreading through you. As you look at the candles on boats that are carrying messages to other people feel the pleasure of knowing the calm they will get from their messages as well.

A relaxation for letting go

Imagine yourself walking along an empty beach. The sun is warm and the sand is clean and smooth. You feel very lucky to be in such a beautiful place on such a lovely day. In front of you, lying on the sand, you spot a small pebble. It is a strange green colour. You bend down to pick it up because it looks so unusual. It is as round as a marble and you roll it in the palm of your hand. It feels soft and yet hard at the same time. It is quite different to any other pebbles you have seen so you decide to keep it. As you carry on walking along the beach you enjoy the feel of the pebble in your hand.

Ahead of you sticking out from the beach into the sea you notice a kind of wall made from large rocks. The rocks are great for climbing over. You clamber along the rocks seeing if you can get right to the end.

After a while of climbing over the rocks you reach the end of the wall and sit down. You look out to sea, getting your breath back after all the clambering you have done. As you sit on the rocks you see a dolphin leaping through the water. It seems to be heading for where you are sitting at the end of the rocks. You watch as it lifts itself up in the water in the way dolphins have and beckons you to join it. The world seems to have become a magical place as you drop into the water and feel yourself supported by the dolphin. You discover that by magic you are able to breathe under the water. Holding onto the dolphin you are taken down to the seabed. The dolphin swims in between two towering pillars made of coral. As you look down you see strange patterns on the floor. The dolphin swims closer to the patterns and you can see that it is a mosaic. There are pebbles and shells, little pieces of rock and coral. They have been carefully placed together to make swirling, whirling, watery shapes. In among the shapes you can see other sea pictures of fish, serpents and sea creatures. Finally the dolphin slows down. It feels as though you are in the very centre of the mosaic. You look down and see a marvellous fish made out of tiny shells. There is just one thing missing. In the space where the fish's eye should be there is just a hole. Suddenly it all makes sense. You remember the pebble. That strange, green, round stone you found on the beach. That is what is missing. At first you close your hand even tighter around the pebble. You think about how unusual it is and how you wanted to keep it for yourself. But then you look again at the mosaic and you realize where the pebble should be. You carefully place it in the space and finish off the mosaic. It is as though all the colours in the mosaic come to life. The shapes and patterns and pictures in the mosaic sparkle and shimmer.

Holding on to the dolphin you swim away. Back you go to the surface where your watery adventure started. The dolphin helps you to climb out and you sit on the rocks letting the sun dry your clothes. As you look into the sea you can see the mosaic shimmering and shining at the bottom of the sea. You feel pleased that you had the missing piece. You feel proud that you were part of making something so very special.

A relaxation for feeling you have something to say

Imagine that you are walking through some woods at the end of the day. You often walk along the path through the woods because the woods feel friendly and peaceful. As you walk you hear a faint crackling sound. You stop and stand still while you try to make out from which direction the sound is coming. Then you catch the smell of wood-smoke. There must be a fire. You peer among the trees to see where the fire is. You spot a small orange glow. The glow does not seem to be getting any bigger or coming any closer, so you decide to see what it is.

As you walk towards the fire you can see it is a campfire. People are sitting around the flames on fallen tree trunks and logs. You stand in the shadows and listen to what is going on. As you listen you realize that the people around the fire are sharing stories. One person after another is taking it in turns to entertain the others with a story. Some of the stories are things that have actually happened to the teller. Other stories are fantasy tales of long ago or far away. Other people tell stories of the future. You listen with such enjoyment to them. You marvel at how different the stories are from each other and how well the tellers spin their tales.

Someone in the group catches sight of you and invites you to join in the circle. It is lovely sitting by the warm fire, watching the flames and the faces and enjoying the tales. However, as you sit there listening, it begins to dawn on you that people are taking it in turns to tell the stories and it is soon going to be your turn. Your mind goes completely blank and you can't think of a thing you could tell them about. You feel worried and anxious. These people have invited you to join them and you have had great fun being with them but now you are going to have to say you can't take part.

Then you suddenly remember a story. It is one you read a long time ago but as you think about it it comes back into your mind.

When it is your turn you start to tell the story you have remembered. You find it quite amazing the way the words just seem to flow into your mind and then out through your mouth. You can tell when you look at the faces of the people listening how much they are enjoying your tale and you become more and more confident. When you finally finish your story you feel triumphant. You are delighted that you had something to tell and you told it so well. You begin to think about other stories and look forward to a time when you will be able to share those with others. To finish off the storytelling there is a feast of potatoes that have been baking in the embers. They taste delicious. You find other people who use the same path as you to get home so you are able to walk with them. As you walk home, notice how confident and pleased you feel and how excited you are about the ideas for stories that you have in your head.

A relaxation to remind you that life is a journey

In your mind's eye picture the top of a mountain covered in snow and ice. The weather is getting warmer and the sun is shining, causing the snow and ice to begin to melt. You can hear the dripping and trickling sound of the ice melting and the water finding a way down the side of the mountain. You see tiny trickles that run together making bigger and bigger trickles until there are small streams of water hurrying over the rocks and down the mountain. Streams meet, getting wider and deeper. The water gushes over rocks making dramatic and exciting waterfalls. The water looks so clear. It sparkles in the sun.

As the stream gets to the bottom of the mountain it meets a small river. The river moves slowly now through the countryside. People are walking along the path by the side of the river. Ducks swim on the river. Sometimes the river runs beneath a bridge and you can see people standing on the bridge watching the water flow by. As the river reaches the town it becomes narrow. Artificial banks make the river deep and dark as it runs between factories. Now there are no birds or people, just dark shadows and damp walls. In the middle of the town the river widens out and becomes a place where people take their sandwiches at lunchtime. People sit by the river enjoying the spring sun. Ducks waddle on the bank hoping to get some crumbs. Swans glide past, graceful and elegant.

You follow the river as it continues to the sea. It travels across wide fields and big open spaces. You see some small pleasure boats on the water where the river widens out to meet the sea. You can see seagulls overhead and hear them calling. The banks of the river are muddy and you see wading birds carefully strutting over the sand and poking their long beaks into the mud, searching for food. You almost don't notice the moment when the river joins the sea. It feels as if one moment you are looking at the mouth of the river and the next out to the huge expanse of the open sea. On the horizon you can make out the shapes of ships heading for other continents. The sky above seems huge.

You remember those tiny drops of water you saw dripping from the end of the icicles high up on the mountain. You feel excited when you think back to the journey you have followed from the very beginning of the river to the sea. You think about the changes you saw in the river, how the same river could flow past so many different scenes before ending up in this vast body of water.

16

Moving on . . .

100 reminders for things you can do when you are feeling stuck

1. Accept the choices your teenagers make if they are able to fund them themselves and able to take the consequences.
   At this point your teenager is taking on the role of an adult. They may need your guidance but they won't need your permission.
2. Acknowledge the help you are given.
   It is all too easy to overlook what other people are doing for you because you are preoccupied with what still has to be done.
3. Be aware of the life other people are having.
   Life can be difficult, but not too far away from you other people are facing up to tricky situations and disappointments too. You are not alone.
4. Be brave when you want to be fearful.
   If you are brave you will look out. If you are fearful you will hide away.
5. Be calm when you want to be angry.
   You are not undermining your case by staying calm.
6. Be compassionate.

When you can see something from someone else's point of view then you enrich your own life as well as theirs.

7. Be creative in small ways.
   Think of something you can do that will cost nothing but will give someone else a lot of pleasure. It doesn't need to take you a lot of time.

8. Be generous when you want to be greedy.
   Let your family have time to explore what they want to do even if what you want them to do is be with you.

9. Be happy for others.
   You will avoid feeling jealous.

10. Be happy for yourself.
    Don't discount the things that you are and that you have.

11. Be strong when you want to be weak.
    See if you can find a safe way of doing something you thought was physically too difficult or technically too complicated.

12. Before you speak check whether what you will say is true, necessary or kind.

13. Check ideas.
    If you hear something that sounds interesting, find out more about it. Look for the complexity in what seems to be a simple idea. Look for the simplicity in what seems to be complicated.

14. Clear your mind when thinking will not help.
    When your mind is racing, focus your attention on anything and you will find that your mind begins to clear.

15. Contribute when you can.

16. Cope with what you can.

17. Curb your impulses.

18. Do something for no reward.

19. Do something for others.

20. Do what you can.

21. Don't be frightened of people.
    If you can approach most people calmly you will be giving them confidence that they can help you.

22. Don't be frightened of pain.
    No one likes pain but the calmer you can be the more you will be able to deal with the pain in yourself and in others.

23. Don't believe criticism is personal.
24. Encourage self-discipline.
25. Enjoy what you can do.
26. Enjoy your age.

    As your children are getting older and stronger you can feel you are getting older and weaker. Look after yourself but don't hanker after times that have passed. Enjoy the times that you have got at the age that you are.

27. Explain things.

    Don't expect other people to know what you need and don't feel miserable when they don't. Give them the courtesy of an explanation and you might be surprised how relationships change.

28. Find something that gives you pleasure near you now.
29. Forgive when you want to condemn.
30. Gather information.
31. Give a compliment when you wanted to complain.
32. Give guidance that isn't criticism.
33. Have faith in your teenager.
34. Have faith in yourself.
35. Ignore irritations.
36. Keep looking after your physical, mental, emotional and spiritual well-being.
37. Keep loving your teenager.
38. Keep your mind open.
39. Know mistakes happen to everyone.
40. Know what you are good at.
41. Laugh when you want to cry.
42. Learn to know yourself.

    Don't take for granted that what you do at the moment is the sum total of what you are. What interests did you have in the past and what would you like to try now?

43. Learn to look after yourself.

    Take time for things that give you pleasure or make you feel fulfilled.

44. Let others live their own lives.
45. Like others.
46. Like yourself.
47. Listen to your teenager.

48. Look for help in yourself or from others.
49. Look for the light inside others.
    Notice where you see the gentleness and when you see the smile.
50. Look for the light inside yourself.
51. Remember that lots of dramas fade quickly.
52. Remember not every disappointment is a catastrophe.
53. Notice the stillness in others.
54. Notice the stillness in yourself.
55. Play fair, be ethical.
56. Play games.
57. Read statements made by the great. They are like food for the mind and the spirit.
58. Relax your mind.
59. Remember teenage life has its downs as well as its ups.
60. Remember we are all doing our best.
61. Remember how you are is how you are seen.
62. Remember you are the adult.
63. Respect experience.
64. Respect others.
65. Say thank you when you want to complain.
66. Decisions about sex are private but people need information.
67. Thinking about sex is part of being a teenager.
68. Share your knowledge.
69. Strengthen your determination.
    When people have felt weak for a long time the temptation is to assume they can only be weak. You can strengthen your determination little by little and reach for the life you want to live.
70. Take only the stress you can.
71. Talk to your teenagers.
72. Remember teenagers can be overconfident.
73. Remember teenagers can lack confidence.
74. Remember teenagers don't have to know what they want to do.
75. Remember teenagers have lots of pressure.
76. Remember teenagers have lots of temptations.
77. Remember teenagers have not had as much experience as you.
78. Remember teenagers may know more than you.

79. Remember teenagers need acceptance even if their behaviour is dreadful.
80. Remember teenagers need guidance to change behaviour that is dreadful.
81. Remember teenagers need to know that what they think is interesting.
82. Notice there are different ways of doing the right thing.
83. Discover there is often nothing wrong with making a wrong decision.
84. Take opportunities to train your attention.
85. Try out new things.
86. Try to be happy.
87. Try to be more tolerant.
88. Try to be positive whatever you do.
89. Try to change fixed attitudes in yourself.
90. Try to increase your level of calm.
91. Try to learn to increase your capability.
92. Try to remember a drama from a week ago.
    You probably won't be able to which just goes to show how quickly we can forget or how quickly normal service is resumed.
93. Try to take delight in the simplest things.
94. Try to think when thinking will help.
95. Widen your horizons.
96. Don't feel a failure just because you are worried.
97. Don't feel rejected because you are not a part of your teenager's life.
98. Give yourself a break – you don't have to compete.
99. Accept that you don't have to have an answer.
100. Vow to stop making judgments about what your teenagers are doing.

Useful addresses

UK

Helplines

Brook Advisory Centres
Tel: 0800 018 5023 (Mon, 9.00–17.00; Wed & Fri, 9.00–16.00)

A free, confidential telephone helpline providing pregnancy and contraception advice.

Brook Helpline
Tel: 020 7617 8000 (24 hours)

Seven information lines of recorded information: emergency contraception; missed periods; abortion; starting contraception; pregnant and unsure; sexually transmitted diseases; what happens when you visit a Brook centre.

Careline
Tel: 020 8514 1177 (Mon–Fri, 10.00–16.00 & 19.00–22.00)

Counselling for children, young people and adults on any issue including relationships, child abuse, bullying, addictions.

Childline
Tel: 0800 1111 (24 hours)

Childline is the free, national helpline for children and young people in danger and distress. It provides a confidential phone counselling service for any child with any problem 24 hours a day, every day.

Contraceptive Education Service
Tel: 020 7837 4044 (Mon–Fri, 9.00–19.00)

Confidential information and advice on contraception, sexually transmitted diseases and all aspects of sexual health.

Drinkline
Tel: 0345 320202 (Mon–Fri, 9.00–23.00; Sat & Sun, 18.00–23.00)

Provides information and advice to anyone concerned about alcohol misuse, including people with alcohol problems and their families, friends and carers.

Families Anonymous
Tel: 020 7498 4680 (Mon–Fri, 13.00–16.00)

A service for friends and families of drug users.

Gingerbread
Tel: 020 7336 8184 (Mon–Fri, 11.00–16.00)

Advice and emotional support for lone parents and their families via a national network of local self-help groups.

Kidscape
Tel: 020 7730 3300 (Mon–Fri, 10.00–16.00)

A registered charity to prevent child abuse and bullying.

National AIDS Helpline
Tel: 0800 567123 (24 hours)

Provides information, support and advice on HIV/AIDS and sexually transmitted infections. The service is confidential and non-judgemental and holds information on local agencies throughout the UK that can provide specialist help.

National Drugs Helpline
Tel: 0800 776600 (24 hours)

Offers confidential information and support to anyone concerned about drug and solvent/volatile substance misuse. Holds information on local agencies throughout the UK that can provide more specialist help.

Parentline
Tel: 0808 800 2222 (Mon–Fri, 9.00–21.00; Sat, 12.00–18.00)

Telephone guidance on parenting issues.

The Samaritans
Tel: 08457 90 90 90 (24 hours)

Telephone helpline and face-to-face service offering emotional support for anyone in a crisis, including those who feel suicidal.

Sexwise
Tel: 0800 282930 (Mon–Sun, 7.00–24.00)

Information for under nineteens.

Websites

www.at-ease.nsf.org.uk
Mental health resource website for young people under stress.

www.bbc.co.uk/so
Magazine-style site aimed at teenagers, including agony aunts, advice, doctors, quizzes, games and revision aids.

www.NetDoctor.co.uk
Information on drugs and alcohol produced for teenagers.

www.pupiline.net
An award-winning website giving advice, news and information on a range of issues concerning teenagers and of interest to young people.

www.thesite.org.uk
Information on drugs. A very useful site as it can give details of local help, based on your postcode, available near you.

www.youngminds.org.uk
A mental health charity for children.

www.youth2youth.co.uk
National helpline for young people under twenty-three.

USA

Helplines

Child Abuse Hotline
Tel: 800 422 4453

National Parents Resource Institute for Drug Education
Tel: 800 279 6361

National Suicide Hotline
Tel: 800 784 2433

National Youth Crisis Hotline
Tel: 800 448 4663

Websites

www.abstinence-ed.com
Training materials to counsel teenagers about sex, pregnancy, abstinence and AIDS.

www.kidshealth.org/teen
Information from the Nemours Foundation. Hundreds of articles for teenagers on health issues.

www.nih.gov
Gives toll free information lines and other telephone numbers that deal with physical and mental health. Also provides information databases.

www.therapistfinder.net
Provides help in finding a health professional in your local area.

Canada

Helplines

National Drug Abuse Hotline
Tel: 800 662 4357

Youth Crisis Hotline
Tel: 800 448 4663

Websites

www.child.net/teenca
Information for teenagers in Canada.

Australia

Helplines

Kids Helpline
Tel: 800 55 1800

Lifeline
Tel: 03 9650 4851

Websites

www.accessinfo.org.au
Information on sexual health.

www.adf.org.au
The Australian Drug Foundation website.

www.eatingdisorders.org.au
Information provided by the Eating Disorders Foundation of Victoria, a non-profit organization which aims to support those affected by eating disorders.

www.friendship.com.au
Award-winning website for young people covering all aspects of friendship.

www.pressurepoint.com.au
Mental health for teenagers.

www.somazone.com.au
Information for teenagers on all aspects of health and mental welfare.

www.thesource.gov.au
Information for young people in Australia.

New Zealand

Helplines

Youth Crisis Line
Tel: 09 376 6645

Youthline
Tel: 0800 376 633

Websites

www.alcohol.org.nz.fuel
The Alcohol Advisory Council of New Zealand provide strategies that will reduce alcohol related problems in young people.

www.trippin.co.nz
Mental health for teenagers.

Marie Stopes International

The charity Marie Stopes International has produced a small booklet aimed at young people giving them information about contraception and the availability of advice concerning pregnancy and sexual health in hundreds of countries around the world. The booklet is called *Your Passport to Sexual Health*, and MSI have also produced a schools edition for pupils going on school trips. This contains practical information for young people to think about before going off without parental guidance. For a copy or further information contact:

Marie Stopes International
153–7 Cleveland Street
London W1P 5PG
UK

Tel: [+44] 20 7574 7400
Website: **www.mariestopes.org.uk**

Index